AF575983

The Kentucky Heritage Land Conservation Fund at Work

Thomas G. Barnes

Acclaim Press
— Your Next Great Book —

P.O. Box 238
Morley, MO 63767
(573) 472-9800
www.acclaimpress.com

Editor: Randy Baumgardner
Book Design: Devon Burroughs
Cover Design: M. Frene Melton

Library of Congress Control Number: 2013922708

ISBN-13: 978-1-938905-46-9
ISBN-10: 1-938905-46-6

First Printing: 2014
Printed in the United States of America
10 9 8 7 6 5 4 3 2 1

Contents

Dedication....4

Acknowledgements....5

Introduction....6

The Kentucky Heritage Land Conservation Fund....7

Resource Management Needs and Issues....9

The Biodiversity of Kentucky....11

Levels of Biodiversity....12

Why Worry....14

HLCF Lands....18

The Future....140

References....141

Index....142

Dedicated to Carl L. Wedekind

June 4, 1926 - July 2, 2011

Carl Wedekind served on the Kentucky Heritage Land Conservation Fund Board from its beginning in 1995 until his death after a short illness, July 2, 2011. Carl served in the Navy Air Corps from 1944-1946, then attended the University of Virginia Law School, graduating in 1950. He returned to his hometown of Louisville and began a 27-year legal career with the firm of Stites and Harbison, including being a partner and managing partner. He left the firm to be the CEO of Kentucky Medical Insurance Company, a major carrier of medical malpractice insurance in Kentucky.

Conservation, civil liberties and abolition of the death penalty were all his causes throughout his career into retirement. In particular, he was an early board member of the Kentucky Chapter of The Nature Conservancy, helping to hire its first staff and managing a successful capital campaign for the fledgling organization. Carl was one of our most faithful and involved members, serving as Vice-Chairman from the beginning and as a valuable, dependable guide for all our actions. We could always count on him to provide sound recommendations and relevant comments for decisions made by the Board. Between Board meetings, I frequently sought his opinion on particular projects and land conservation issues in Kentucky.

In the last few years and until his death, he was quietly pursuing independent, private funding from across the state to provide long-term, sustained support of the KHLCF. As a member of the Board's Project Review Committee, he loved to visit the lands that the Board was going to consider for funding. This photograph of Carl was taken on one of the more recent of those site visits. His stamp of approval meant that an area was a part of Kentucky's natural heritage that deserved protection for posterity. He was a model for all conservationists to follow in our effort to protect Kentucky.

In memory of his long, productive life and devotion to conservation in Kentucky, the Kentucky Heritage Land Conservation Fund Board dedicates this book.

We miss you greatly, Carl.

William H. Martin, founding Chairman
Kentucky Heritage Land Conservation Fund Board

Acknowledgements

This book project has been going on for what seems like forever. Consequently, I will undoubtedly leave someone out who needs to receive credit for assisting me, supporting me, and heck, even aggravating me.

I am very thankful to my two Forestry Department chairs, Dr. Steve Bullard and Dr. Terrell "Red" Baker, for the unwavering support of this project and my program in the Department of Forestry. I am very grateful for the HLCF Chairman and board for supplying me with the funding to visit sites and for the publication of the book. This group of fine individuals had the patience to wait, to help review the manuscript, and even listen to me drone on about the project at more than one of their meetings.

To Joe Dietz and Bill Martin, thanks so much for your assistance and support of all aspects of this book, from the original concept to the completion of the final product, which you hold between your hands.

To those who assisted me in the field like Morgan Jones, owners (or managers) of the county and city properties, and field technicians for the various agencies, without your assistance this book would have never been completed as you were instrumental in getting me information, directions, or assistance in the field and made being outside in the wilds a pure joy, particularly for those areas that I had not visited prior to working on this book.

To the staff in the HLCF office, who were very kind in their assistance in getting file folders with information and direction to sites and for being very kind and thoughtful in finding me a desk to work at, conversation, and general help in getting things organized.

Zeb Weese did an amazing amount of work after I had completed my portion of the book and he assisted me while working for the Kentucky State Nature Preserves in visiting sites under his management, taking me to locations after his appointment to the HLCF biologist position, and then in writing and providing photographs for the sites I had not visited.

To the folks at Acclaim Press, especially Doug Sikes, publisher and Randy Baumgardner, managing editor, for their support of this project and my other book projects. I am also thankful for the wonderful staff at Acclaim Press who does the editing, layout, design, marketing, and other aspects of publishing a book.

Finally, I need to thank my family and friends who have supported me over the years.

Introduction

We as human beings have a capacity for and can be quite benevolent and affectionate when it comes to caring about nature, but we can also be incredibly contemptuous, ignorant and oblivious to where we fit into the natural world and how our actions impact the natural world. As a human species in this country, we are rapidly becoming separated from nature and unknowingly or unwittingly accept that we can, quite literally, change and reshape the land to fit our demand for cheap resources, whether it is energy, water, wood or food. We lead such consumptive lifestyles, thinking little of the environmental repercussions, and we can no longer live with an unattainable reality that true economic progress will continue if we persist to use and exhaust our, and our children's, natural resources capital as if it were some expendable surplus commodity to be used like it will always be abundant and readily extractable.

Wendell Berry summarizes this idea as he states in the preface of the book, *Kentucky's Natural Heritage*: "…have had sufficient time and opportunities, we have failed to develop an effective culture of land stewardship…the economy of Kentucky has no connection with the land of Kentucky. This is the definition of an economic ignorance that is conventional, criminal and suicidal." In short, Wendell is saying we have failed to develop a land ethic described by Aldo Leopold over 60 years ago.

There is no doubt that Kentucky is a beautiful state with a diversity of rural environments including mountains, streams, lakes, forests, fields and swamps. In terms of rural land conversion and protection, Kentucky ranks number 47 in the amount of public land, and all the surrounding states have protected more land for conservation than Kentucky.[1] A Natural Resources Conservation Service report showed that Kentucky loses more than 105 acres of rural land every day as a result of land conversion.[2] Furthermore, we rank 5th highest in the projected amount of rural land that will be converted to other uses in the future.[3] We have the 7th highest wetland loss in the country, and over 81% of all wetlands in the state have been destroyed.[4] Overall, approximately one-half of one percent of Kentucky is in some form of pre-settlement vegetation[5] and as I stated in Kentucky's Last Great Places, we have essentially lost the bluegrass savanna ecosystem, less than 1% of bottomland hardwood forests remain intact, most of the forests have been cut two or three times and we have less than 10,000 acres of old growth forest, and of the 2 to 3 million acres of native grasslands, a few thousand acres remains. In terms of specifically protecting land for the conservation of biodiversity, one state agency, The Kentucky State Nature Preserves Commission, who is charged with this task, has only protected 0.001% of the land base of this state. Even with the conversion of wild lands to other uses, the state still has beautiful landscapes of fields and forests. Since 1994, a program was initiated to allow the state and local governments to acquire land for posterity so that future citizens and visitors can continue to enjoy the beauty and natural resources in the state. This program, the Kentucky Heritage Land Conservation Fund, was established by the legislature in an initial effort, although small by many standards, to protect land for conservation.

Kentucky is a beautiful rural state that has a diversity of habitats ranging from mountains to southern swamps. This sunrise over the Cumberland Plateau was taken from an overlook on the Kentucky Department of Parks Pine Mountain Trail in Harlan County with funds provided by the Kentucky Heritage Land Conservation Fund.

The Kentucky Heritage Land Conservation Fund

The Kentucky Heritage Land Conservation Fund was established by the Kentucky Heritage Land Conservation Act of 1990 (KRS 146.570), and the money has been protecting land since 1995. This book is a celebration and recognition of the lands purchased by Kentucky Heritage Land Conservation Fund. These lands are significant and noteworthy, and on the 15th anniversary (1995-2010), more than 120 properties in 67 counties totaling more than 85,000 acres have been protected. These lands range from protection of the 13th largest old growth forest in the eastern United States, to one of the largest urban forests in Jefferson County, to green space and walking trails in Owensboro, to the palisades and cliffs of Central Kentucky. It has protected lands important for conserving biodiversity, providing for recreational and or outdoor educational activities, habitat for songbirds and other species, and land that would be lost to "development" if not protected.

What exactly is the Kentucky Heritage Land Conservation Fund? Quite simply, it is a mechanism for collecting money from the sale of the "nature" license plates, the state portion of the un-mined minerals tax, environmental fines and interest income, which is used exclusively for the purchase and management of conservation areas in Kentucky. A twelve-member board, seven appointed by the governor representing specific entities such as the Kentucky Academy of Sciences and five ex-officio state agency personnel, oversees the fund and its disbursements. The board employs professional biologists and administrative staff to oversee the program, which is administrated by the Kentucky Department for Natural Resources. On average over the past five years, the Kentucky Heritage Land Conservation Fund balance receives approximately $5.24 million annually with the largest source of income coming from the un-mined minerals tax and environmental fines. This figure can vary tremendously

The initial nature license plate of the Kentucky Warbler was released in 1995.

The Bobcat license plate.

The second set of nature plates, released in 2003, replaced the original Kentucky Warbler plate.

The third set of nature plates was released in 2008.

from year to year, with the unpredictability and volatility of the environmental fines. One constant source of revenue is the sale of the "Nature's Finest" license plate, which generates around $750,000 annually.

Out of the total budget, the Kentucky Environmental Education Council receives $150,000 to further their mission, which is to help Kentuckians develop the skills necessary to solve current environmental problems, prevent new ones, and maintain a balance between the economy and the environment for future generations. By statute, the Department for Energy Development and Independence receives $400,000 annually, with the expressed purpose of providing public education of coal related issues annually.

Remember the Smiley face license plate that was unveiled in 2002 and available in 2003? It was not a hit and was replaced in 2005. At the same time, three new Kentucky's Finest Nature plates, the bobcat, cardinal, and viceroy were released and the original Kentucky warbler plate was allowed to expire, which was first released in 1995. This stroke of luck gave motorists the opportunity to have a high quality nature plate showing their concern for the outdoors instead of the smiley face plate on their vehicle. By the end of the second year of distribution of the new plates, 1 in 20 vehicles had a Nature's Finest plate. The third round of plates featured a hummingbird, dragonfly, or Cumberland Falls.

Since the Kentucky Heritage Land Conservation Fund receives approximately $5 million a year in revenue, you would think this is a tremendous amount of money. But when it comes to land acquisition, it is like a rain droplet in the proverbial barrel. For example, in 2010, one 453 acre tract purchased by the Kentucky State Nature Preserves Commission with Kentucky Heritage Land Conservation Fund cost $1 million and change. In addition to actually purchasing the land, the money is also issued for doing the title search and most importantly, 10% is set aside for management costs associated with purchasing the land. Nonetheless, even though this amount of funding is small, it is significant because it is the only source of income for purchasing land by a variety of state agencies. The Kentucky Heritage Land Conservation Fund recognizes this fact and its mission statement reflects this: "the primary source of state funding for the purchase of natural areas and is committed to protecting and conserving our Commonwealth's precious natural areas for enjoyment by this and future generations." The Kentucky Heritage Land Conservation Fund Board produces an annual report that provides transparency on the fund and highlights revenue and expenditures for that fiscal year. In addition, the report contains more information on specific properties that were purchased and a complete listing of all purchased projects since the inception of the program.

Half of the proceeds of the fund are disbursed to five state agencies: Department of Fish and Wildlife Resources, Department of Parks, Division of Forestry, Nature Preserves Commission, and Kentucky Wild Rivers program. Each of the agencies receives 10% of the funding or in total, one-half of the revenue. The remaining 50% of the funding is open to local governments, colleges or universities, other public agencies, or nonprofit land trust organizations. In order to qualify for funding, the project must fall under at least one of four priorities:

- Natural areas that have unique attributes and qualities for the protection of rare, threatened or endangered species;
- Areas important for migratory birds;
- Areas that perform natural functions subject to alteration or loss;
- Areas preserved in their natural state for public use, outdoor recreation or education.

There is an application and process for obtaining funding, and the original application must have the priority or priorities that the proposed project addresses, costs associated with purchasing the property, how the 10% management funds will be used, and a preliminary resource management plan. Properties can only be purchased from willing sellers, and they cannot be purchased for more than their state appraised value. If the project is approved, the recipient has two years to actually close on the property and they then have to conduct biological and archaeological inventories and submit those with a final resource management plan no later than two and one-half years years after purchase. After purchase, the properties are also subjected to periodic visits by Kentucky Heritage Land Conservation Fund staff to ensure appropriate management is being followed.

The most important components of the final resource management plan are the biological and archaeological inventories. In general, it is difficult to manage natural resources if you do not know what is present to manage, and it provides an opportunity for the "discovery" of new rare plant or animal occurrences, as in the case of Wood's false hellebore at the Kentucky State University environmental education property or the discovery of a new species, the melon- or cucumber- vine, at the Livingston County Wildlife Management Area.

Resource Management Needs and Issues

Conservation of natural resources is a management system of ensuring that habitats and the components of those habitats are maintained in a natural state that remains steady resisting unnatural change. At the broadest levels, it involves not only preservation, keeping in an unaltered state with little to no human activities occurring on the site, to active management or manipulation that will modify the environment to meet human defined goals. All management decisions, even those where no decision is made, have impacts on the system that are positive, negative, or neutral in their effects on the habitat. Almost every habitat has been altered to some extent by human activities, directly or indirectly, and it is therefore imperative that natural lands are managed to achieve some desired habitat condition.

Management can be as simple as marking boundaries or as complex as conducting a prescribed burn. The first step in the management process is to inventory the ecological communities and living organisms present, in addition to the nonliving components like soils, etc., to facilitate conservation planning. Conservation planning directs specific management activities and the implications of those activities for conserving biodiversity. Inventories are essential for conservation planning because they document the occurrence, distribution, and abundance of plants and animals at a particular location. For example, say biologists find a rare plant growing in a sensitive environment, like a particular orchid growing in an acidic, stream-head wetland. Once this information has been generated it may direct conservation planning to close the area to public use because of site sensitivity (in advertent habitat alteration from trampling, off-road vehicle or horse use) or because the orchid is highly desired and could be poached. Furthermore, once the habitat is delineated other management issues can be discussed relative to maintaining a viable habitat for the species. In the case of the orchid it could be management to maintain the hydrology of the site and to remove vegetation to keep the site open and reduce competition with woody plants.

Invasive Species are undoubtedly the biggest problem on all lands that the Kentucky Heritage Land Conservation Fund has provided funding to acquire. The enormity of this issue can't be over stated. Invasive species cost this country more than $100 billion annually[6] and the ecological impacts, not easily quantified, can be staggering. There are no economic data for the impact of invasive organisms in Kentucky, but you do not have to look far to see their impact. One only has to drive from Lexington to Louisville or Cincinnati to see how bush honeysuckle has completed taken over the forests in this part of the state altering forest composition and productivity for decades. Think about the economic impact on just forestry with the impacts of chestnut blight, emerald ash borers, hemlock wooly adelgid, thousand canker disease (walnut) and several approaching problems including Asian longhorn beetles and gypsy moths. Each property purchased by the Kentucky Heritage Land Conservation Fund has its own set of unique invasive problems ranging from Japanese stilt grass to autumn olive to tree-of-heaven. The most common invasive species that need management attention on these properties include Queen Anne's lace, yellow and white sweet clover, Japanese honeysuckle, bush honeysuckle, multiflora rose, garlic mustard, common chickweed, musk thistle, silky lespedeza, tall fescue, beefsteak, winter creeper, tree-of-heaven, royal princess tree, privet, Japanese knotweed, Japanese chaff flower, Chinese yam, and johnson grass. The hemlock wooly adelgid is also a serious invasive problem on several properties that have hemlock dominated communities including Blanton Forest, Bad Branch State Nature Preserve, etc.

The second largest management issue on these lands is human recreational activities and management. With an ever increasing human population it is getting more difficult to manage natural resources to benefit the resource, and not humans. For example, the illegal access of use of the properties by off-road vehicles presents serious problems on multiple properties. This is problematic because of the problems associated with unwise ATV use includ-

Controlling invasive species are the top management issue on many of the HLCF lands.

ing soil erosion or compaction, creating an avenue for invasive plants to spread, destruction of native plants and vegetation, loss of wildlife habitat and increased stress and disturbance of native wildlife, and increased air and surface and ground water pollution through sedimentation and other factors. In other cases, managing human activities includes restricting access from cliffs and climbing, or entering caves which can be defaced or infected with white-nose syndrome which is killing native bats. Another example of management activities might include the creation and maintenance of walking, hiking, or biking trails and roads to provide recreational opportunities for people. Finally, some properties have developed infrastructure such as disabled accessible trails, gazebos, weather stations, interpretive areas or signage to assist users in learning and understanding the features of the environment.

Naturally set fire has been an integral component of numerous ecosystems including Pine Barrens, grasslands, and even some forest types in Kentucky. Managers are now using prescribed fires in an attempt to manage or restore those ecosystems that need fire. At the same time, some ecosystems, particularly the rich forests, did not require fire to maintain the ecological integrity of the system.

One of the more important management activities is to monitor rare plants and animals. This must occur to evaluate the efficacy of management decisions to determine if the organisms are still present and whether their populations are increasing or decreasing as in the case of this state special concern Eastern Ribbon snake which has had a tag implanted in it so that it can be monitored with a scanner.

THE BIODIVERSITY OF KENTUCKY

When I wrote *Kentucky's Last Great Places*, which was published in 2002, I thought I had been to many of the state's outstanding natural areas. Since that time and another ten years wandering around Kentucky, I have discovered that I barely touched the surface of exploring this great state and its natural areas and biodiversity.

As a state, we have much to take pride with respect to our biodiversity. The Kentucky State Nature Preserves published a book in 2010 entitled, *Kentucky's Natural Heritage*,[5] that highlights the biodiversity of the state and in doing so they point out that Kentucky has 30% of the total species of North American fish, 35% of the North American mussel or freshwater clam species, 26% of the salamander fauna, and 10% of the world's crayfish or crawdad species. This certainly makes sense because we have more miles of navigable water than any state in the country except Alaska. In addition, they report that there are 102 species, subspecies or varieties of plants and animals that are found in Kentucky and nowhere else in the world. To top it all off, we have a diverse geology that gives rise to a large number of caves like Mammoth Cave, and unique cave organisms, and we have the second or third most number of natural arches or bridges of any state in the country with more of them being found annually. However, biological organisms continue to face pressures from a variety of sources and we now have a new federally endangered species in the state, the Cumberland Darter. Kentucky has the 9th highest number of plant and higher animal extinctions, is 10th in percentage of mammals that are at risk of extinction, 15th in percentage of freshwater fish at risk of extinction, and 2nd in the percent of freshwater mussel that are imperiled in southeastern US.[7]

While the Kentucky State Nature Preserves Commission, Daniel Boone National Forest, Mammoth Cave and Cumberland Gap National Historical Park, and Kentucky Department of Fish and Wildlife Resources protect much of the rare biodiversity in the state, some of Kentucky's biodiversity has been protected on properties purchased with Kentucky Heritage Land Conservation Fund money. For example, the Green River is recognized nationally as an ecologically important river for the protection of aquatic biodiversity, and Kentucky Heritage Land Conservation Fund has helped purchase numerous land holdings that are adjacent to, or drain into, this watershed and help conserve this unique river system. The great thing about the Kentucky Heritage Land Conservation Fund program, is that unlike programs from the Kentucky State Nature Preserves Commission or The Nature Conservancy, this program has the ability to protect biodiversity in general, or protect species that may not be rare or endangered, but also those species that are common like white-tailed deer, viceroy butterflies, cardinals, or rainbow darters. It is beyond the scope of this book to showcase all the biodiversity of the state, the 2010 book Kentucky's Natural Heritage, does a much better job of doing that. This book will highlight the biodiversity of Kentucky Heritage Land Conservation Fund properties that not only protect rare species and habitats, but also more common species.

What is this biodiversity that we are trying to conserve? Biodiversity quite simply is the biological web of life, this great inter-connection of all things living and the physical environment that supports the living web. Every single organism has some role to fulfill in this complex web of life and while we still do not completely understand everything, we do know that you cannot continue to remove species without affecting something else which then affects something else and you end up with this snowballing effect and at some point the web falls apart. Natural systems are dynamic and may tolerate disturbance but the conservative approach is to protect all the parts to ensure a healthy environment for future generations such that they have the same possibilities previous generations had for sustainable use and appreciation of renewable natural resources.

The uncommon Baltimore checkerspot was found during an inventory at a Kentucky Heritage Land Conservation property purchased by a county fiscal court in southern Kentucky.

Levels of Biodiversity

Biodiversity occurs at all biological levels, and it is important to understand that protecting the genetic diversity of a species or population is just as important as protecting a species or ecosystem. Take for example the small white prairie lady slipper orchid. This species is considered secure, but it has been extirpated from Missouri, New Jersey, Pennsylvania, and Saskatchewan and is considered rare in 12 of the 16 states in which it is known to occur. The normal habitat for this species is moist to wet prairie and calcareous fens and in Minnesota, which has the largest and most secure number of populations, it has declined by 95%.[8] The southern edge of this plant is in Kentucky, and it grows in a unique habitat called a limestone slope glade. These are quite unique in that they have thin soils and occur on hot, dry south facing slopes with scattered limestone ledges and outcroppings with stunted trees. They can be moist in the spring but then dry out in the summer and become almost like concrete they are so hard. As our globe continues to heat up, and precipitation events become more unpredictable and droughts more inevitable, perhaps the Kentucky populations of this species harbor the genetic material to ensure the survival of this species throughout its entire range because they are already adapted to hot, dry conditions. Hence protection of this genetic material is important and one outstanding natural area in Kentucky was expanded with funding from Kentucky Heritage Land Conservation Fund to protect one of the best populations of this plant in the state.

The next general level of biodiversity is the species level and most of us inherently recognize a species like a cabbage butterfly, a robin, a hemlock tree, etc. So how many species can be found within Kentucky's borders? We really do not know an accurate number, but we do know it is conservatively around 19,400, which does not account for things like fungi, lichens, lower animals like worms, bacteria and other microorganisms. Of this number, we have approximately 15,000 insect species, 2,500 plant species, 380 mollusks, 370 birds, 245 fish, 67 mammals, 54 reptile and 53 amphibian species.

While it is easy to increase species diversity by simply disturbing any natural community, this ultimately diminishes the native biodiversity at least in the short term and potentially the long term. Why? Because the native species are often displaced by early successional weedy or exotic species that can outcompete the native plants and alter the plant community permanently. In some cases, the exotic species can ultimately diminish native biodiversity. Take the hemlock wooly adelgid, an invasive organism that will kill our hemlock trees. So what if we lose our hemlocks? What impact will losing this one species have on other species in the ecosystem? Numerous studies have found that the loss of the hemlock will result in an entirely different plant community that will replace the hemlock forest, and the new forest will most likely be dominated by tulip tree in sites where large leaf rhododendron is not present. In addition, invasion by tree-of-heaven, Japanese stilt grass and other invasive species will increase, which further diminishes native biodiversity. Furthermore, recruitment of a new hemlock forest will be difficult in the future as advanced regeneration and seed banks have minimal hemlock retained in the plant community. The loss of hemlocks has been shown to alter plant and bird communities along with soil processes and hydrological regimes. The loss of these trees along streams will affect both macro-invertebrate and fish species, particularly those that require cool water habitat. This is just the tip of the iceberg, as we are now just beginning to do the science to find out exactly how devastating the loss of this species is and that is why several Kentucky Heritage Land Conservation Fund properties have chosen to "treat" selected hemlocks and spare them in hopes they will provide the foundation for a new hemlock forest.

The final general level of biodiversity is the different ecosystem types found across the landscape. Kentucky is home to at least 62 different ecological communities including forests, prairies, glades, cliffs/rockhouses, forested wetlands, swamps, wet grass wetlands, marshes, seeps, ponds, rivers, and lakes. Kentucky is blessed to have one of the most diverse deciduous temperate forest ecosystems in the world, the mixed mesophytic forest. Within this ecosystem type a number of different plant communities oc-

The small white lady slipper orchid grows in an atypical habitat of a limestone slope glade. Because this species occurs in a hot, dry environment, it may harbor the genetic material for preservation of this species. The largest population of this species in the state was protected by the Kentucky State Nature Preserves Commission on a preserve that was purchased with the assistance of funding from the Kentucky Heritage Land Conservation Fund.

cur and range from dry-acid pine-oak forests to cove hardwood forests where no individual tree species dominates the plant community. Slope, aspect, and geology all affect which plant and animal communities occur in this forest ecosystem. In addition, smaller communities like cliff-lines or semi-bogs or gravel cobble-bars along major drainages, add to the diversity in this ecosystem. The Kentucky Heritage Land Conservation Fund has protected a wide variety of ecosystem types from the mixed mesophytic forests of Eastern Kentucky to the Kentucky Barrens or Meadows to the cypress-tupelo swamps of western Kentucky.

The sand hill crane is an example of species diversity and is the most easily understood level of biodiversity by the general public.

A riparian forest is an example of ecological community diversity shown here in the spring at the Lower Howard's Creek Preserve with sycamore and redbud as the highlighted trees.

Why Worry

Why should we, average Kentucky citizens, worry about protecting biodiversity? The short and simple answer is that we human beings absolutely, positively rely on it for our very existence from the air we breathe, to the water we drink, to the food we consume, to the medicines we take, to the inspiration it provides for arts and music, for the opportunities to educate our children and future generations, and to the faith, values, and morals that bind us together as human beings. In Kentucky, biodiversity "goods" and services are intrinsically linked to our forestry or wood production valued at $6,4 billion[9], our tourism industry valued at $11.3 billion,[10] hunting, fishing, and wildlife associated recreation valued at $1.8 billion,[11] agricultural crop and livestock sales valued at $4.2 billion,[12] and untold value for other industries in the state. A couple of specific examples will illustrate this point from a purely utilitarian viewpoint on how important protecting biodiversity is for Kentucky.

The first value is related to the medicines we take to keep us healthy. The common Kentucky woodland wildflower, bloodroot, has been used to produce the drug Sanguinarine, which is used as a dental plaque inhibitor and as a feed additive in swine, bovine, and poultry diets to decrease amino acid degradation, increase feed intake, and promote growth. The mayapple, common in Kentucky forests and fields, contains chemicals that are the precursor to two semi-synthetic cancer drugs, Etoposide and Tenisopiside. Etoposide is used to treat lung cancer and Kentucky has the highest lung cancer rate in the United States.[13] A conservative estimate is that 4,482 Kentuckians have lung cancer every year and the typical chemo treatment costs using etoposide as one ingredient cost $8,300[14], which means that it cost Kentucky $3.72 million annually to treat this deadly disease. Tenisopide is used to treat lymphoma and leukemia after other treatments have often failed. In terms of the economic impact of medicines we take, one single study has documented that plant based medications sold over the counter and via prescription have sales of over $84 billion annually. Add to this the value from the medicinal/herbal trade and the total sales top at over $108 billion annually.[15] It is estimated that at least 25% of all pharmaceuticals are plant derived. What if we destroy plant species without ever screening them for their potential medicine benefit?

We really don't think much about food in this country, but we should. It might surprise some people to realize that 75% of man's food need is met by consuming just twelve species of plants and five mammals or birds.[16] Amazingly, 75% of the world's agricultural genetic diversity has disappeared in the last century. Perhaps you did not know that selected plant breeding, using wild stocks and other sources, was responsible for half the gains in agricultural productivity from 1930 until 1980?[16] Think about how one species that is declining, the honeybee, is responsible for pollinating 70% of the world's food crops. This can be seen on a spectacular level when discussing corn. Corn is the number one cash agricultural crop in Kentucky and is grown on approximately 45% of cropland in the state. It is used for feeding livestock (25% goes to feeding chickens alone), bourbon and other distilled spirits, food and other products, ethanol, and for export. The value of the 2010 corn crop according to University of Kentucky Agricultural Economists was $830 million.[12] Over

Bloodroot, a common Kentucky wildflower, has been used for medicinal purposes in addition to being a livestock feed additive and is found on multiple properties purchased with funding from the Kentucky Heritage Land Conservation Fund.

The sand grape is a species of native plant, listed as state threatened, that was and continues to be a root stock for commercial grape production.

thousands of years, scientists have bred high-yielding, disease resistant corn varieties that have low genetic diversity. In 1970, a leaf fungus attacked 15% of the nation's corn crop by a leaf fungus. Farmers lost over $2 billion almost overnight, and it was a primitive ancestor to the corn plant that held the genetic key to creating blight resistant corn. In an era when we look to other "crops" to supplement declining tobacco revenues, some farms have shifted to growing grapes for wine and other uses. In the late 1800's, the root stock of four Native grape species, two that occur in Kentucky and are listed as rare or threatened, saved the grape industry from an aphid outbreak. Finally, we can look to one of our native woodland species, the walnut, which provides disease-resistant root stock for the commercial walnut industry valued at over $1.1 billion in 2010.[17] In summary, the value of agriculture to this state's economy exceeds $4.2 billion annually.[12] This reality underscores and highlights how humans are more dependent, not less dependent even with advanced technologies, on nature and the services it provides.

People are a component of ecosystems, and we depend on a variety of ecosystem functions to keep us healthy, wealthy, and wise. Stable, biologically diverse ecosystems perform vital ecosystem services that humans need to survive. Ecosystem services are made up of various functions related to habitats, and biological or system properties that are performed by ecosystems. Ecosystem goods and services like food or waste assimilation are the fruits of those ecosystem functions. A recent paper in the prestigious scientific journal *Nature* by R. Costanza and others at the University of Maryland has broken ecosystem services into 17 categories that include gas regulation, climate regulation, disturbance regulation, water regulation, water supply, soil formation, nutrient cycling, erosion control, waste treatment, pollination, biological control, refugia, food production, raw materials, genetic resources, recreation, and cultural, and they conservatively estimate the average annual economic value of these is an outstanding $33 trillion!

Perhaps the final utilitarian value is from insurance prospective or what is called the precautionary principle. We do not know what will happen in the next decade, century, or far in the future. As global climate change continues to alter our biosphere, and species, habitats, and ecosystems are lost, degraded, or altered, we need to purchase an insurance policy to protect

Each species is important in the web of life and provides stability and integrity to the system, just as each intersecting point in a spider web does the same thing.

Six Mile Creek borders the environmental education Center at Kentucky State University. One of the most important ecological values provided by protecting biodiversity is clean water, which provides safe drinking water for most urban Kentucky citizens and habitat for aquatic species such as fish and fresh water mussels, our largest group of endangered animals.

us from an uncertain future. This goes back to the spider web analogy. We are all linked together, and losing a single point in the web will not likely cause the entire system to collapse, but how many can be lost without the system collapsing? It is also a question of legacy and what type of world we will be leaving to future generations. What is our responsibility to future generations and who decides? I have been extremely fortunate to have seen wild grizzly bears, and wolves, and eagles and rare orchids as have my children. Who gave us the permission to determine whether future generations get to see polar bears outside a zoo, or see a white prairie lady slipper orchid, or understand that there really was a walnut tree and to discover that it was destroyed by an exotic organism and Walnut is not just the name of a street in the city? I know I would have loved to have seen the vast migration of passenger pigeons and not just poke around pigeon roost creek, which was undoubtedly named for the vast numbers of pigeons that roosted there.

But there are also intrinsic reasons, not related to use or economic benefit, for protecting biodiversity. All major faith traditions in the world have statements regarding the wise stewardship of the earth's resources. While largely ignored for years, many faith traditions today have observed the ecological crisis unfolding in our lifetimes, and are renewing or initiating programs to promote sustainable resource use as a function of morals and ethics with respect to the creatures and other organisms with which we share the earth.

American Bald Eagle, *a uniquely American symbol, has made a comeback with the elimination of some toxic pesticides, and now nests in Kentucky at several locations with funds used by the Kentucky Heritage Land Conservation Fund for purchasing the property.*

Richard Louv, in *Last Child in the Woods*, contends that we have nature deficit disorder and that direct exposure to nature is "essential for healthy childhood development and for the physical and emotional health of children and adults." We have lost our connection to the natural world and seem to rely on this exposure through indirect contact via the arts and humanities, via photographs, paintings, music, writing, poetry, etc. Many students entering natural resource programs at Universities today get an interest in the outdoors by watching Animal Planet, National Geographic Channel, or the Discovery Channel. So in a very real sense, protecting biodiversity is the bridge that provides the inspiration for these activities until new generations can get that direct exposure to nature and appreciate it.

This is just a short synopsis of why we should protect and conserve natural resources and biodiversity. It is certainly possible to write an entire tome on the subject but the essential point is, protecting biodiversity is important and Kentucky Heritage Land Conservation Fund is one mechanism that can help achieve the goal of protecting some of Kentucky's unique biodiversity.

Flat Lick Falls in Jackson County was purchased with a wide variety of funding from various sources, and the County is looking to purchase additional acreage in the gorge below the falls with HLCF funding. This popular site is now owned and managed by the county, and hiking trails and an outdoor toilet have been installed to make the property more accessible.

HLCF Lands

Lower Howards Creek in Clark County was one of the first sites protected by HLCF and several other purchases by HLCF have increased the acreage substantially.

Adkisson Greenbelt Trail

City of Owensboro, Daviess County, 25 acres in 12 tracts

This linear park is designed to provide for outdoor recreation and link neighborhoods, parks, schools, and businesses along its 15-mile length. The Greenbelt Trail of over 15 miles follows the creek winding through agricultural fields, neighborhoods, and business districts. Creek bank vegetation is typical and dominated by sycamore, black cherry, green ash, cottonwood, and silver maple. Several small ponds are located in the Greenbelt.

Access: The trail is open dawn to dusk and no motorized vehicles or horses are allowed. It is open to pedestrians and bicyclists and meets American with Disability standards with a 10' wide asphalt path. Accessible at various locations including New Hartford Road, E. Byers Avenue, Higdon Road, and Old Hartford Road.

Overlooking a small pond adjacent to the Greenbelt Trail.

Apple Valley Glades

Kentucky State Nature Preserves Commission, Bullitt County, 69 acres

This site protects a series of dolomitic limestone glades interspersed with cedar-oak woodlands and sub-xeric calcareous forest. The glades are open, exposed bedrock surrounded by thin, gravelly soils and are the primary habitat for the globally rare Kentucky Glade Cress. This little mustard is only known from Bullitt and Jefferson Counties, and populations in the last decade have declined by more than 75% as a result of the loss of habitat due to development pressures. There is sparse vegetation on the glades, which is dominated by annual dropseed. In the thin soils surrounding the exposed bedrock, little bluestem, tall dropseed and curly or poverty grass dominate with a handful of wildflowers including bastard toad flax, prairie tea, pale purple coneflower, gaura, St. John's wort, several blazingstars, hoary puccoon, false aloe, rosepink and Leonard's skullcap.

In addition to the gladecress, other rare species found here include the state threatened ringseed rush and state special concern Crawe's sedge. The woodlands are dominated by red cedar and post oak, with some small trees like southern buckthorn, redbud, persimmon, blue ash, sassafras, and winged elm interspersed. The sub-xeric calcareous forest serves as a buffer to the glades, and typical trees found in the canopy include shagbark and pignut hickories; white, chinquapin, and black oaks; sugar maple; serviceberry; hackberry; white ash; and slippery elm; with an understory of Carolina buckthorn and prickly ash. The herb layer is sparse with flowers, although sedum, rue anemone, goldenseal, Solomon's seal, and Christmas fern do occur here. More than 200 plant species have been documented growing here.

Access: Due to site sensitivity and private ownership, this preserve is not open to the public.

Apple Valley Glades provides habitat for the Kentucky Glade Cress, which helps protect this species from extinction.

Archer-Benge State Nature Preserve

Kentucky State Nature Preserves Commission, Whitley County, 1,864 acres
Text writtten by Zeb Weese.

This preserve is the eighth state nature preserve on Pine Mountain, and protects a significant portion of one of the largest forest blocks in Kentucky. It spreads across the north and south faces of Pine Mountain in Whitley County, and is so remote locals have referred to it as "South America" for over a century because you can't get there from here. This inaccessibility has helped maintain the integrity of the ecosystem to an amazing degree.

The KHLCF partnered with several organizations, including the US Fish and Wildlife Service, the Kentucky Natural Lands Trust, and the estate of Dennis Benge, to protect this unique large forest block. Even though the site was logged in the 1960's to mid 1970's, and mid to late 1990's, the stream, Laurel Fork, has been largely un-impacted and is the real gem on this property. Rare species abound in Laurel Fork stream, including the state endangered Michaux's bluets and another state threatened aquatic plant species and multiple rare mussels and fishes. Rare mussel species known from Laurel Fork from the Kentucky/Tennessee state line to near Frakes include the only known Clear Fork watershed records for the Cumberland elktoe, a federally endangered species endemic to the upper Cumberland River system and another endemic species, the Cumberland Papershell.

Recent surveys have documented approximately 25 species of fishes from the mainstem of Laurel Fork, including several rare and endemic fishes. Rare species include the federally threatened Blackside Dace, the Cumberland Darter, which is an endemic species that is extremely rare, remaining in only 15 streams in Kentucky, and Cumberland Arrow Darter, endemic to the upper Cumberland River system. The portion of property located on the north side of the mountain is rich and moist and supports a mesophytic forest that is typical for Pine Mountain's north face dominated by tulip tree and eastern hemlock.

Several karst features have been explored along the north face and a small colony of federally endangered Indiana bats has been documented as well as an endemic cave beetle. On the southerly-facing dry slopes of Pine Mountain, Appalachian sub-xeric forest is most common forest type on the preserve dominated by oaks, hickories and red maple. A similar community, the acidic xeric forest/woodland is a more open, drier forest with thin, often rocky soils where the bedrock is often exposed. Here, sun-loving grasses and forbs are more abundant. Along the upper slopes near the summit, a few massive rock outcrops occur and the Cumberland Mountain xeric pine woodland/outcrop community occurs. This woodland has little herbaceous cover but the vegetation, especially shrubs and small trees dominated by Virginia and Pitch Pine and xeric oaks, occur in scattered in places where soil has developed.

Several state special concern plants, pale corydalis and Appalachian rosinweed have been observed in these areas. There are five major drains that contain dense rhododendron thickets, as well as several large sandstone exposures and rock shelters. The deeper ravines are dominated by a hemlock-mixed forest. This preserve was named in honor of Hugh Archer, founding director of the Kentucky Natural Lands Trust and the late William Dennis Benge, a private citizen whose love of nature led him to bequeath substantial financial resources towards the purchase of this large forested block at the base of Pine Mountain

Access: Due to rare species and access issues, the site is not currently open to the public.

Late summer wildflowers at the edge of Laurel Fork stream. Photo by Mark Evans, Kentucky Natural Lands Trust.

John James Audubon State Park

Kentucky Department of Parks, Henderson County, 662 of 1,377 total acres

Audubon State Park is the home of the famed naturalist, ornithologist and painter, and the park museum features the largest collection of original Audubon art in the world in addition to personal artifacts about his life. The surrounding forest along the bluffs of the Ohio River is mature, almost old growth in nature with some trees more than 200 years old. Approximately half of the property has been dedicated as a state Nature Preserve. At least 61 species of trees and more than 200 wildflowers have been documented from the site.

The north facing, mesic forests are dominated by American beech, sugar maple, and American basswood, whereas the more south facing slopes are dominated by sugar maple, various oaks, and tulip tree. At least 169 bird species have been observed in the park. The purpose of purchasing the 13-acre Pritchett tract was to prevent development along the highway from encroaching onto the existing state park lands. A 650-acre wetland linking the park to the Ohio River was recently purchased with help from the Southern Conservation Corporation; a biological inventory has not been conducted yet but the site is known to have a bald eagle nest and heron rookery, as well as habitat for waterfowl and amphibians. Plans are underway by the Friends of Audubon, a local nonprofit, to make the wetland handicap accessible through a series of boardwalks.

Access: More than 6.5 miles of hiking trails are available for use from dawn to dusk and one short trail is available for dog walking. Off-road vehicles and horses are prohibited. There are other forms of recreation, such as camping, available at the park. The entrance is on the east side of US Highway 41 between Walnut Lane and Stratman Road, Henderson.

Blue-eyed Marys and wild ginger carpet the forest floor at Audubon State Park.

Axe Lake Swamp State Nature Preserve

Ballard County, Kentucky State Nature Preserve Commission, 312 of 7,458 total acres

This nature preserve is one small part of a 3,500-acre cypress-tupelo swamp and bottomland hardwood forest system that is considered the largest in the state. It is considered an important component of the North American Waterfowl Management Plan, and thousands of wintering waterfowl, particularly wood ducks, can be found at the site. The largest portion of the preserve is in cypress-tupelo swamp with an understory of buttonbush and swamp privet. Another component is bottomland hardwood swamp dominated by river birch, sweet gum, cottonwood, red maple and oak, with little herbaceous layer due to inundation by water much of the year.

A very small portion, which delineates the Ohio River floodplain, is coastal mesophytic forest dominated by maple, sweetgum, sycamore, hickory and oak. More than 153 species of plants, eight mammals, seven amphibians, and 49 birds have been documented. This is the only known location for breeding great egrets in the state. Three state listed fish including the endangered cypress minnow and threatened red spotted sunfish and Lake chubsucker; three state listed plants including the threatened water hickory and Carolina fanwort, and special concern snow melanthera; one state listed amphibian, special concern green tree frog, and one state listed mammal, the special concern evening bat, are found on the preserve.

Access: No public access except with written permission or on guided field trips by KSNPC staff due to fragile resources and limited parking. Axe Lake is adjacent to the Boatwright Wildlife Management Area.

Green tree frogs are a state special concern species and occur in a dozen or more western Kentucky counties where they are associated with forested wetlands, particularly cypress swamps like Axe Lake Swamp.

Cypress Trees are abundant at Axe Lake Swamp.

Bad Branch State Nature Preserve

Kentucky State Nature Preserves Commission, Letcher County, 853 acres in three tracts out of 2,639 total acres

This is one of Kentucky's premier nature preserves situated deep in the heart of the Cumberland Mountains. E. Lucy Braun, noted ecologist, first recognized the importance of this area in the late 1930's at a time when there were at least five moonshine stills operating in this remote area. Shortly after she visited and documented the ecological importance of the site, it was extensively logged in the 1940's. This preserve was one of the first dedicated nature preserves in the state, with the purchase of 435 acres in 1985.

Total acreage of the preserve is now 2,639 acres and includes most of the Bad Branch watershed, which was named a Kentucky Wild River in 1986. The elevation ranges from 1,760 to 3,000 feet and four general forest types; dry Appalachian forest, dry pine-oak forests, mixed mesophytic forest, and hemlock forest in the ravine, occur on the preserve. This diversity of habitat types, differing slope and aspects, and forest types makes this a diverse preserve and more than 230 species of vascular plants, 51 lichens, 23 liverworts, 133 mosses, 8 algae, 35 diatoms, 54 birds, 28 mammals, 15 fish, 25 amphibians, and 15 reptiles have been found.

Unique attributes of this preserve include a 60-foot-tall waterfall, enormous sandstone cliffs, a hemlock dominated gorge, and a cold, fast-moving mountain stream. This preserve hosts one of the largest concentrations of rare plants and animals in Kentucky, and includes the only nesting site for common ravens on the cliffs; a rare fish, the federally threatened blackside dace; and numerous plants including painted trillium, small enchanter's nightshade, matriarch's grape fern, Canada burnet, Southern heartleaf, Curtis' goldenrod, Red-twig doghobble, Rock harlequin, White walnut, Small sundrops and unique high-elevation southern Appalachian species like Fraser's sedge and Michaux's saxifrage.

Rare species found on the addition purchased with HLCF funding include Steele's joe-pye-weed, showy gentian, painted trillium, kidney leaf tway-blade, and two mammals, red-backed vole and cinereous shrew. The gorge forest is dominated by large hemlock trees and the associated forest is typical mixed mesophytic with tulip tree, Fraser magnolia, American beech, yellow and sweet birch, yellow buckeye, and American basswood with an understory of rosebay rhododendron, flowering dogwood, and sweet pepperbush. Forest types above the gorge are typical Appalachian dry and pine-oak forests dominated by chestnut, white, black and scarlet oaks with Virginia, pitch and short-leaf pine with sourwood, serviceberry, red maple, and sassafras as understory trees. The shrub layer is dominated by ericaceous shrubs, with native grasses and herbs at the ground level.

Management: The primary management concern is the introduced Wooly Hemlock Adelgid. Because of the significance of the hemlock in maintaining the ecological integrity of the gorge forest, more than 15,000 hemlock trees have been treated with insecticides. This treatment will need to be continued for an extended period of time, because treatments only last three to five years. Other management issues include maintaining hiking trails and remediating damage from illegal off road vehicles that encroach and travel on the preserve, and control of exotic invasive plant species.

Access: The preserve is open daily from sunrise to sunset, and is accessible via 7.4 miles of hiking trails rated strenuous. The gravel parking area is located approximately 2 miles east on the left side of US 119, 8.0 miles south of the junction of KY 15 and US 119 in Whitesburg.

Scarlet red blueberries and huckleberries carpet the rocks at High Rocks at Bad Branch State Nature Preserve, which is the highest point on Pine Mountain.

Baker Natural Area

Logan County Conservation District, 66 acres

Located in the heart of the "Big Barrens" region of central and western Kentucky, this natural area is an excellent example of remnant grassland and glade ecosystem nestled within an oak hickory forest complex. The grassland vegetation is dominated by various prairie grasses, including big bluestem and Indiangrass on deeper soils and little bluestem on more shallow soils. The plant community is diverse and over 375 species of plants have been documented. The grassland wildflowers are showy throughout the summer months and include the glade and narrow-leafed coneflower, black-eyed susans, button and spiked gay feather, various sunflowers, and several rare species including cut-leaf prairie dock, Carolina delphinium, purple prairie clover and chestnut sedge. The site also includes several small limestone glades, a place where the limestone bedrock comes to the surface, and unique species like prickly pear cactus, widow's cross, and slender heliotrope can be discovered growing it appears almost out of the rock.

The forest, which covers approximately two-thirds of the area, is dominated by six species of oak and three species of hickory. The conservation district has put in a loop walking trail for public access. They also constructed a small pond, weather station, and bird blind at the north end for environmental education programs such as Envirothon. The Logan County Conservation District was awarded a KHLCF Stewardship Award in 2012 for their work on the Baker Natural Area.

Access: Open to the public from sunrise to sunset daily. Parking is available at the north end where the trail begins. The property is located at the corner of Sportsman Road and the north Bypass on the northwestern corner of the city of Russellville.

A field of pale purple and glade coneflowers flowering at the back of the Baker Natural Area.

Big Rivers Wildlife Management Area and State Forest

Kentucky Division Forestry and Kentucky Department of Fish and Wildlife Resources, Union and Crittenden Counties, 6,800 acres. Written by Zeb Weese.

For over two decades this site was owned and operated by a timber company, Kimball International, under management practices for sustainable forestry developed by the Forest Stewardship Council. The KHLCF worked with The Nature Conservancy and the United States Forest Service Forest Legacy program to acquire Kimball's property at the confluence of the Ohio and Tradewater Rivers. The management area includes several miles of Ohio River frontage, which has lost over 50% of its riparian forest habitat along its entire length to development.

Nearly 4.5 miles of the Tradewater River is also protected here on both banks; the Tradewater is the only free-flowing tributary of the Ohio River in the Commonwealth. The site includes habitat for several federally listed species, including the copperbelly water snake, Indiana bat, gray bat, fat pocketbook mussel, piping plover, and the interior least tern. The Kentucky Department of Fish and Wildlife Resources also anticipate breeding and restoring fat pocketbooks at the site, as well as the state-listed alligator gar. The Big Rivers site is directly across the Ohio River from the 277,000-acre Shawnee National Forest in southern Illinois, which is designated a "source forest" for native bird populations by the Central Hardwoods Joint Venture. This means that the survival of many of our native songbirds depends on the health of this large habitat block.

The diverse ecological communities here include the state-imperiled wet bottomland hardwood forest, which is dominated by swamp white, cherrybark, and bur oaks; the xerohyridic flatwoods, a globally imperiled community dominated by post, blackjack, southern red oaks; and over 200 acres of palustrine wetlands, 80% of which have been lost in Kentucky. The site is managed for hiking, hunting, fishing and paddling, and the area has received an Outstanding Remarkable Value designation for recreation and scenery by the National Park Service.

Access: From Sturgis, take KY 109 north for 1.2 miles, then a slight left onto KY 1508 for 1 mile. There are several parking lots and access points on the left, including a boat ramp for the Tradewater.

Red Shoulder hawks are common in the forests of this region of Kentucky.

The red eared slider is a common turtle in the wetland areas at this wildlife management area.

Blanton Forest State Nature Preserve

Kentucky State Nature Preserves Commission, Harlan County, 1,635 of 3,124 total acres

This is the largest old-growth forest in Kentucky, and it protects five natural communities on the south face of Pine Mountain. While some trees in protected coves along Watt's Creek can approach three to five feet in diameter, many of the over 300-year-old trees are much smaller because they are growing on thin soils on the south face of the mountain. In addition to the forested communities, this preserve also protects large cliffs and rock outcroppings, large rock shelters, and unique Appalachian acid seeps dominated by various sphagnum mosses, cinnamon ferns, and various wildflowers. Over 400 species of plants have been noted from the preserve and include three rare mosses and the state special concern spinulose wood fern.

The federally threatened blackside dace occurs in Watts Creek, and other rare animals noted include several rare insects, the state threatened common raven, and state special concern Kentucky red-backed vole and cinereous shrew. The most diverse forest found at Blanton is the Appalachian mesophytic forest which occurs in ravines, coves, and sheltered slopes. These forests are dominated by hemlock, tulip tree, white oak, basswood, sugar maple, American beech, and sweet birch with other species including yellow buckeye, cucumber tree, black gum, white ash, bitternut and shagbark hickory and northern red oak. The understory is also diverse and dogwood, spicebush, umbrella and Frasier's magnolia, American holly, serviceberry, maple leaf viburnum, pepper bush and hydrangea abound and in some areas the large leaf rhododendron forms dense, almost impenetrable thickets. These sites support a rich spring flora with wood anemone, bloodroot, speckled wood lily, false Solomon's seal, yellow mandarin, dwarf crested iris, wild geranium, baneberry, foamflower, blue cohosh, and various violets. In steep ravines, the forests are almost completely dominated by hemlock and large leaf rhododendron.

The upper, drier sites support Appalachian sub-xeric forest dominated by chestnut oak, white, northern red and black oak, pignut hickory, red maple, tulip tree, black gum, and pitch pine. The upland dry sites are primarily pine-oak forests dominated by pitch, shortleaf and Virginia pine, scarlet and chestnut oak with blueberries, huckleberries, and mountain laurel in the understory. The Appalachian open acid seeps typically form at the head of a stream and feel spongy when walking on them because of the large amount of sphagnum moss that sits on the surface over the water/soil mixture. These habitats are dominated by alder and winterberry, with turtlehead, Canada lily, cinnamon and New York fern, meadow beauty, and zigzag goldenrod. There are both dry and moist sandstone cliffs and rock outcrops, and they are dominated by various ferns, mosses, and lichens and in some cases wildflowers where cracks and depressions develop. The dry sites have bracken, mountain spleenwort and polypody ferns, mountain laurel, alumroot, and wintergreen in these areas whereas the moist sites have fragile, lady, cinnamon, royal, filmy, hay-scented and maidenhair spleenwort ferns, bishop's cap and partridge berry.

Access: Open dawn to dusk to the public via foot traffic only on the 4.5 miles of trails. Take US Highway 119 approximately five miles west of the city of Harlan and turn north on KY 840 at a sign for Camp Blanton. Follow KY 840 for approximately two miles, and the parking area for the preserve is on the right adjacent to Camp Blanton.

Under the canopy of large, old growth American beech and Eastern Hemlock trees at the upper end of the Watts Creek trail where some of the largest trees grow in Blanton Forest.

Blood River State Nature Preserve

Kentucky State Nature Preserves Commission, Calloway County, 193 acres

What a spectacular place for the Kentucky State Nature Preserves Commission to dedicate as its 60th preserve. One of the rarest ecological communities found in Kentucky, the coastal plain forested acid seep is only found in Kentucky, Illinois, and Tennessee. Groundwater percolates up through sand and gravels to create a permanently wet, saturated soil habitat that is dominated by various ferns including cinnamon, royal, and netted chain ferns, on a bed of sphagnum moss. The seeps are surrounded on the uplands by dry, acidic forests along the hills dominated by white, black, scarlet and southern red oaks as well as pignut hickory.

Downslope towards the Blood River, the habitat changes to seasonally or permanently wet bottomland hardwood forests dominated by water tupelo, black gum, sweet gum, and red maple with subordinate species including green ash, swamp chestnut oak, and American hornbeam. The site provides habitat for numerous rare species including the state listed piedmont azalea, possum haw viburnum, prickly bog sedge, and weak stellate sedge. Within the larger Blood River ecosystem habitat is provided for state listed plants such as the threatened mock bishop's weed and Nutall's oak, and several state listed animals including the Blood River crayfish, three-lined salamander, and western mud snake.

Federally endangered gray bats are known from the area, and a large great blue heron rookery is nearby. The site is adjacent to a TVA property that will prevent development, but the surrounding area is subjected to pressure from siltation from logging and farming activities and hydrological changes associated with nearby Kentucky Lake.

Access: Due to site sensitivity of the site, this preserve is not open to the public.

Cinnamon fern at the edge of the seep and the toe slope indicates saturated soil conditions at this small wetland.

This is the only known location for the Piedmont azalea in Kentucky.

Blue Licks State Park and Short's Goldenrod State Nature Preserve

Kentucky Department of Parks and Kentucky State Nature Preserves Commission, 1,114 acres in five tracts

Blue Licks State Park is known for the Battle of Blue Licks, which was the last battle of the Revolutionary War fought by Daniel Boone and other frontiersmen on August 19, 1782 after Cornwallis surrendered at Yorktown, Virginia in 1781. It is also known historically for the salt and mineral licks that attracted large numbers of American bison and European settlers.

In the late 1700's, settlers would boil water from the area for several days to make salt, which was used to season meats and preserve food. They could boil enough water in two days to make sufficient salt to last Fort Boonesboro an entire year. But the salts were also an important mineral for the American bison that would migrate to the area by the tens of thousands, and in 1800 it was reported that the hills were devoid of vegetation and looked like a desert as a result of the concentration of these large bison herds. The actual pounding of the earth by these massive mammals, in addition to mastodons and woolly mammoths of times past, created a well worn trace into the soil that is still visible today and along which Short's goldenrod is found.

Short's goldenrod is a federally endangered plant that only occurs in a two-mile radius around Blue Licks and was originally discovered at the Falls of the Ohio in 1840 by Dr. Charles Wilkins Short, a noted botanist and professor of medicine at Transylvania University and the Medical College of Louisville. That population was destroyed when McAlpin Dam was constructed in the 1920's and was rediscovered in the Blue Licks area by E. Lucy Braun in 1939. It was considered a Kentucky endemic until 2001, when it was rediscovered in Indiana. The goldenrod was intimately associated with the bison and the soil disturbance they created.

The original park was established in 1927, with 37 acres and protected a common grave for 60 of Daniel Boone's men. Additional acreage was purchased in 1951, 1986 and 1996, bringing the total park acreage to 177 acres. In the 1970's, a campground was constructed and some of the best short's goldenrod habitat was destroyed and in 1981 the original bison trace was protected as a state nature preserve. The land purchased by KHLCF funds included bottomland agricultural fields adjacent to the Licking River and several important ecological communities including limestone glades, post-black jack oak barrens and woodlands, and early successional calcareous forest. All these habitats have the potential to support populations of Short's goldenrod.

Pre-sunrise overlooking the Licking River with Blue Licks State Park and Nature Preserve to the left of the river.

More than 155 species of plants have been documented in the park. The limestone glades have shallow to very-shallow, well-drained gravelly soils that support early successional grasses like tall dropseed, broomsedge, several three awns and purple top with red cedar, redbud, flowering dogwood, and rusty blackhaw as woody associates. The barrens and woodlands have varying degrees of canopy closure, with dominant species including post, blackjack, white, southern red, and black oak, white ash, pignut hickory, American persimmon and fringe-tree. Early succesional forests on lower slopes are dominated by white ash, black walnut, tulip tree, slippery elm, hackberry, black cherry, white and Chinquapin oaks, and American elm. Upper slope canopy species include shagbark and pignut hickory, white ask, white, Shumard, shingle and black oak, hackberry and red cedar with an understory of rusty blackhaw, common prickly ash, devil's walking stick, rough-leaf dogwood, flowering dogwood and sassafras.

Management: Because Short's goldenrod prefers natural disturbance and invasive exotic plants are a serious problem on disturbed sites, most of the management is concentrated on dealing with crown-vetch encroaching from the highway right of way, as well as Queen Anne's lace, garlic mustard, common chickweed, musk thistle, white sweet clover, tall fescue and Japanese honeysuckle. Additional management includes the monitoring of rare the plants, Short's goldenrod, state endangered yellow gentian, and state threatened Great Plains Ladies Tresses and trail maintenance.

Access: There are multiple parking areas to the park on US 68 near the Nicholas/Robertson County line. The park is open dawn to dusk with foot traffic only on the trails. The Fleming County acreage is currently closed to the public due to endangered species protection.

Short's goldenrod at Blue Licks Battlefield State Park and Nature Preserve.

Boatwright Wildlife Management Area

Kentucky Department of Fish and Wildlife Resources, Ballard County, 1,177 of 8,389 total acres

This wildlife management area is designed to protect and enhance winter waterfowl populations and is an important site of the North American Waterfowl Management Plan. The primary habitats found include cropland and wetland and 39% is classified as wetland, 34% as open land, 17% forest and 10% open water. Wetland habitats include old oxbow lakes, marshes, and cypress swamps. There are also created moist soil wetlands in addition to natural wetlands. Some bottomland hardwood reforestation has also been done. Much of the habitat can be under water during the winter season and provides important habitat for bald eagles, several gull species, and waterfowl. One tract adjacent to the Ohio River provides nesting habitat for the interior population of the least tern, a federally endangered shorebird.

Access: Open to fishing, boating and hunting, although some parts of the area are closed from October 15 through March 15 to serve as a refuge. Other tracts are open and waterfowl blinds are available by advanced application. No access is allowed when flooding prevents access to the blinds. All terrain vehicles and horseback riding and the collection of plants or animals are prohibited. From Wickliffe, travel north on US 51 and turn right onto Gum Corner, Swan Lake Road, or East Cairo Road.

Snow geese congregating on their migration northward in corn stubble located on private land adjacent to the Boatwright Wildlife Management Area which provides nighttime roosting habitat.

Swamp mallow at the edge of a cypress pond at the Boatwright Wildlife Management Area.

Bouteloua Barrens State Nature Preserve

Kentucky State Nature Preserves Commission, Lincoln County, 261 acres

Located in the outer bluegrass region of central Kentucky, this natural area is an excellent example of limestone prairie and is probably the largest remaining grassland in this part of Kentucky. This natural area is a matrix of old fields, native prairie, cedar thickets, and young forest. The preserve gets its name from the state special concern grass species, side-oats grama (*Bouteloua curtipendula*) which is found in abundance on this site. The native prairie is dominated by various prairie grasses including little bluestem, big bluestem, Indiangrass, prairie three awn and several dropseeds. Typical grassland flowers found include gray goldenrod, rosinweed, orange coneflower, wild bergamot, slender lespedeza, prairie tea, bastard toad flax, green antelope horn milkweed, white blue-eyed grass, hairy lespedeza, gaura, and flowering spurge. State listed plants in addition to side-oats grama include special concern species Crawe's sedge, Eggleston's violet, and round-headed bush clover, and state endangered hairy false gromwell. In addition, French Grass, not really a grass but a showy blue wildflower, a declining species has also been found. More than 198 plant species, 39 butterflies and moths, 149 birds, 7 mammals, 5 amphibians, and 2 reptiles have been observed using the preserve. A rare moth, thought to be extinct from the 1800's, was discovered in 2009. The other habitats occurring on the preserve include tall fescue old field with some native prairie species present, red cedar thickets, and young dry to moist calcareous forest and thickets with a mixture of black walnut, black cherry, bitternut hickory, hackberry, white ash with some pockets of blue ash, chinquapin, bur, Shumard and post oak, Ohio buckeye with an understory of rough leaf dogwood, Carolina buckthorn, redbud, sugar maple and rusty blackhaw.

Access: No public access except guided field trips by KSNPC staff due to fragile resources and active resource management.

Side-oats grama grass is named Bouteloua and hence this name was given to this preserve because of the abundance of this native grass at this location in the Outer Bluegrass Region.

Native prairie grasses (the barrens) on the ridge in front of the forest at first light at Bouteloua Barrens State Nature Preserve.

Breckinridge County Wildlife Education Park

Breckinridge County Fiscal Court, 25 acres

This site is an environmental education demonstration area. An old field was converted to native warm season grasses to serve as a buffer area for the adjacent park. The field was seeded to big bluestem, Indiangrass, little bluestem, and switchgrass.

Access: Open dawn to dusk for passive recreation only, and there are no trails for public access. In addition, visitors should be aware the property borders the local sportsman club's shooting range and should avoid access during times when there are active shooting events. Located off Kentucky Ave or Bishop Lane, Irvington.

Late evening after sunset overlooking the native grass plantings at the Breckinridge Wildlife Education Park.

Brigadoon State Nature Preserve

Kentucky State Nature Preserves Commission, Barren County, 92 of 184 total acres

Brigadoon State Nature Preserve is an excellent example of mature to old growth forest that remained in a single family for more than 180 years. The land was part of a 1000-acre land grant to John Renfro at the end of the Revolutionary War, and the site had no commercial logging although selected trees were felled for family use. The original 92-acre nature preserve was purchased from the Nature Conservancy in 1985 and the acquisition of three additional tracts with HLCF funding and a bequest from the former owner almost doubled the size of this site.

Brigadoon is a grade quality B mature to old growth western mesophytic forest that is bordered on the north side by Barren River Reservoir. The ravines and deep soil forests that gently descend to the lake are the most diverse on the property, and are dominated by northern red oak, white ash, walnut, sugar and red maples, hackberry and tulip tree. The upland forests are dominated by tulip tree and American beech. In addition, there are several young successional stands of eastern red cedar and eastern white pine in small patches. The preserve is more than 70% forested with several fields reverting back to forest that are dominated by briers, blackberries, sassafras, sumac, and thistles. The north facing slopes have a rich spring wildflower display with trillium, celandine poppy, dwarf crested iris, jack-in-the-pulpit, hepatica, dutchman's breeches, yellow trout lily, rue anemone, bishop's cap and Virginia bluebells. More than 170 species of plants have been documented on the preserve. In addition, this preserve provides excellent habitat for birds as more than 103 species have been observed.

Access: Open from dawn to dusk for passive recreation including hiking, bird watching, nature photography, etc. No horses, mountain bikes, or ATV's allowed. Follow US 31E south for 6.5 miles south of Glasgow and turn left onto Dover Church-Browning School Road. Go approximately 1.5 miles and turn left onto Mutter Road. The parking area is approximately one-half mile on the left.

Blue phlox and spring beauties are part of the diverse spring flowers found at Brigadoon State Nature Preserve.

Broke Leg Falls

Menifee County Fiscal Court, 15 acres

Once upon a time, music played late into the night, and there was dancing and dining. The restaurant fed tourists and locals alike, and the nine cabins provided comfortable lodging for tourists. What were they coming to see? An outstanding natural feature located just ten miles south of Frenchburg called Broke Leg Falls. The main attraction was the 60' waterfall that dropped over the cliff into a narrow gorge below. At the time it cost a dime to gain entrance to see this natural wonder with an interesting name, "Broke Leg Creek and Falls".

How did it get this name? The folklore surrounding the name is that an ox was gored and broke a leg and then was swiftly carried by the water over the cliff into the gorge below. But then hard times came to the park and once the Bert T. Combs Mountain Parkway was completed in the 1960's, the area lost its commercial appeal as tourists no longer travelled the curvy roads, and the state lost interest in roadside parks and put their resources into developing rest areas and amenities along the interstate highways and parkways throughout Kentucky. Ultimately, the infrastructure fell into disrepair.

Today, the buildings have been removed and the stairs and railings descending into the gorge have been repaired and visitors can once again experience this beautiful setting. There are two sets of falls on the creek. The upper falls is more of a small cascade or series of cascades, and the lower falls drops over the cliffline into a narrow hemlock dominated gorge with typical mixed mesophytic forest species like tulip tree, white oak, northern red oak, sweet birch and several different magnolia species. The cliff faces have a diversity of mosses, liverworts, and ferns and more 279 species have been identified in the park. Stream quality is rated good, with 19 species of fish observed including one sensitive species, the redside dace. There appears to be some issues with ATV use upstream outside the park property, as three species of fish able to tolerate degraded water quality conditions were documented beneath the falls. More than 18 amphibians, 3 reptiles, and 38 birds were observed. Although the site suffered extreme damage from a tornado in March of 2012, there is a well-maintained walking trail that leads from the parking area across the creek, over the top of the waterfall to a series of concrete steps that lead the visitor down the gorge.

Access: Open to the public from dawn to dusk daily. Parking is available at the gravel lot located adjacent to US 460, 10.8 miles south of Frenchburg. Watch for a sharp turn and turn left onto the short paved road, which leads to the parking lot. The trail begins at the east side of the parking lot.

Lower Broke Leg Falls drops more than 60' into a forested gorge.

Buck Creek Nature Preserve

Pulaski County Fiscal Court, 35 acres

This small preserve of mature forest purchased from The Nature Conservancy is located in a sea of recently harvested forest and open agricultural lands and was purchased to protect water quality in Buck Creek, which is an outstanding resource water with 73 species of fish and 30 species of mussels occurring throughout the creek. There are two significant mussel beds that occur adjacent to the property, and several endangered mussels can be found in these beds including the federally endangered Cumberland Bean and the state endangered purple Lilliput and Tennessee clubshell. Two additional rare mussel species, the federally endangered Cumberland combshell and state endangered fluted kidneyshell, are found very close to the preserve as are state special concern sedge wrens and Henslow's sparrows in the uplands. The state special concern Northern White Cedar is located at one corner of the preserve. The upland forest is dominated by American beech, eastern hemlock and white oak with an understory of mountain laurel, which is unique considering the location of this preserve.

Access: Open dawn to dusk via foot traffic only on the hiking trail. From US 27 go to Kentucky 70 in northern Pulaski County and turn to the east traveling approximately 5.3 miles to KY 485, then turn north for approximately 1.9 miles on Goochtown Road (KY 485). Turn right (east) onto Goodhope-Goochtown Road and follow for approximately one-half mile, crossing Buck Creek. The parking lot will be immediately adjacent to the creek on the left.

Yellow trillium, star chickweed, golden ragwort, and blue phlox in flower near Buck Creek on the Buck Creek Nature Preserve.

Burnett Watershed and Wildlife Conservation Area

Located on the Little South Fork, Kentucky Division of Water Wild Rivers Program, Wayne and McCreary Counties, 1,900 acres. Written by Zeb Weese.

The Burnett Watershed and Wildlife Conservation Area protects almost two and one-half miles of the Little South Fork and not only provides access for fishing and passive recreation, but also protects several rare species of mussels including the federally endangered palezone shiner and Tennessee clubshell. Other state listed species found on the preserve include the Illinois pondweed, which only occurs in pools associated with good quality free-flowing water, and Rafinesque's big-eared bat. Diverse ecological communities are found on the site, including Appalachian mesophytic forest, Appalachian subxeric forest, acidic xeric woodlands, xeric Virginia pine woodlands, dry sandstone cliff, mesic/wet sandstone cliff, calcareous mesophytic forest, calcareous sub-xeric forest, xeric calcareous woodland/forest, and riparian forest. Tree species diversity includes American beech, black walnut, cucumber tree, black cherry, several oaks, basswood, and yellowwood. Common shrubs are flowering dogwood, witch hazel, spicebush, streambank mock orange, and maple leaf viburnum. The herbaceous understory is lush and diverse in the lower elevation coves and include spotted geranium, sharp lobed hepatica, Mayapple, bloodroot, and Allegheny spurge. The bird life is diverse and the forest provides nesting habitat for many warblers, including the Blue-winged warbler, Cerulean warbler, ovenbird, Kentucky warbler, Louisiana waterthrush, and Hooded warbler. The highlight for hikers is the trail to "the Pilot", a knob that sits 600 feet above the river and provides outstanding views of the valley below.

Access: Open to the public by foot traffic only, no ATV or horseback riding, and overnight camping and campfires are prohibited within 30 feet of a wild river. Hunting and fishing are allowed according to state law. From Monticello take KY 92 East for 10 miles, then right on KY 1756 for 3 miles, then continue on Parmleysville Road for 1 mile, then Griffin Rice Mt Road for 0.3 miles, then Steele Hollow Road for 1 mile. After you cross the Little South Fork on a metal bridge you are on the property – parking is just up the hill.

View from the top of the cliffs looking west. Photo by Zeb Weese.

Camp Nelson Civil War Heritage Park

Jessamine County Fiscal Court, 268 of 535 total acres

Camp Nelson, located in the rolling hills of central Kentucky near the palisades along the Kentucky River to the south and west and Hickman Creek on the east, was founded in June 1863 when the Union held most of Kentucky. It became an enormous base of operations for the Union Army, and was located on more than 4,000 acres with more than 300 buildings. It became a major quartermaster depot, recruitment and training center, and hospital. It was the third largest recruiting, mustering and training center for African American troops in the nation. All the buildings and structures, except the Oliver Perry house, were dismantled and sold after the base was closed. Several historic sites are located in the park including Fort Jones, which was a redoubt or an enclosed fort built to protect a position from all sides, and the 10' tall earthen embankments still remains in addition to two stone small stone forts that were used to defend the Hickman valley and were made on the edge of the cliff.

This portion of the park includes a small part of Kentucky River palisades and provides habitat for the state special concern Svenson's wild rye, cliff-melic grass, and federally endangered gray bats. The forests along the palisades are young and have serious issues with invasive plants. The riparian forests along the river and creek are dominated by boxelder, sycamore, white elm, green ash, walnut, hackberry, and Ohio buckeye with silky dogwood, spicebush, and witch hazel in the understory. Typical herbs include wild rye grasses, wood nettle, violets and white snakeroot. The moist forests on the lower slopes are dominated by sugar maple, but a variety of other species also occur in the canopy including Ohio and yellow buckeye, American basswood, black walnut, hackberry, blue and white ash, northern red, Shumard, and chinquapin oak. The understory is dominated by spicebush and bladdernut. The dry upland forests are dominated by blue ash, chinquapin and Shumard oak, red cedar, sugar maple, buckeye, and rock elm. More than 352 plant species, 9 mammal, 15 amphibian, 16 reptile, and 91 bird species have been observed. There is also a nature center and convention facility that is a double pen log house built prior to 1825, with a modern addition that can handle up to 75 people.

Access: Developed trails are open dawn to dusk to foot traffic only, and pets must be on a leash. Take US 27 south of Nicholasville 6 miles just past the turn off to Kentucky Highway 1268 (Sugar Creek Pike). Turn onto original Danville Pike to the entrance, which is approximately one mile north of the national cemetery on US 27.

Old split rail fence leading to a lone maple tree on the ridgetop at the Camp Nelson Civil War Heritage Park.

Carpenter Cave

Kentucky State Nature Preserves Commission, Allen County, conservation easement 14 acres

Located along the Barren River, this cave has a rich history of use dating back to early 1800's, when a blacksmith by the name of Carpenter located his home on a cliff above the cave. During the war of 1812, the cave was used as a source of making salt peter, the principal component of gunpowder, and the remnants of the vats the miners built to leach nitrate salts can still be found in the cave. The site was considered a popular destination for spelunkers in the past, as well as a community gathering location in the early 1900's. All these disturbances had a dramatic impact on the number of bats using the cave.

Since the current landowners have taken control of the property and installed an alarm system, no unauthorized entry has occurred. This has resulted in the number of federally endangered gray bats increasing from 700 to more than 17,000. The cave entrance lies on the western side of the Barren River and fortunately is above flood levels. There is also a spring above the cave entrance. The forest surrounding the cave is mostly calcareous mesophytic and sub-xeric, with a diverse assemblage of plants. The mesic sites are dominated by sugar maple, white ash, northern red oak, pignut hickory, American basswood, slippery elm, and sycamore with an understory of American hornbeam, spicebush, Carolina buckthorn, and wild hydrangea. This forest also has a rich and diverse spring wildflower display of trout lily, wood poppy, blue phlox, purple phacelia, stonecrop, scrambled eggs, bellwort, spring beauty, mayapple, and wild ginger. The more upland sites are drier and dominated by red and sugar maple, mockernut hickory, tulip tree, American beech, and chinquapin oak with a sparse understory with service berry, flowering dogwood, sourwood and farkleberry. More than 160 species of plants have been observed on the property including the state special concern white walnut.

Access: Due to site sensitivity and private ownership, this preserve is not open to the public.

Purple phacelia and blue phlox at the entrance to Carpenter Cave.

Carter Caves State Resort Park

Kentucky Department of Parks, Carter County, 107 of 1,600 total acres

This important acreage serves as a link between the park and Tygart's State Forest to form a continuous forest area of more than 2,500 acres. The property begins with the cliffines and rock outcroppings from Smokey Lake and runs northwest, giving rise to two primary forest types: one on southwest slopes and the other on northeast slopes. The southwestern slope forests are dry to moist and dominated almost exclusively by white oak, with black oak and pignut hickory of secondary importance. The northeastern slopes are more mesic, but are mostly young forest dominated by tulip tree with white oak, sugar maple, a few hickories and elm. The cliffline and rock outcropping plant communities are dominated by sugar maple, chinquapin oak, blue and white ash, American basswood, northern red oak, and American elm. There is one large open fescue field in the center of the tract.

The forest understory is not well developed and has a decent spring wildflower display of yellow lady slipper orchids, shooting star, large white trillium, bloodroot, foamflower, wild geranium and jack-in-the-pulpit. More than 175 species of plants can be seen, including the state endangered limber honeysuckle, which was rediscovered from historical records near this site, and the state threatened downy arrowwood. One cave that harbored several federally endangered Indiana bats was also found at this site. Finally, the federal candidate Allegheny wood rat was found.

Access: The park offers hotel style rooms in the lodge as well as cottages and cabins and space for tent camping. A variety of recreational opportunities are available including golf, fishing, canoeing, and cave tours in addition to hiking trails. ATV's and off-road vehicles are not allowed. Take I-64 to exit 161 and drive 1.5 miles on US 60 east to KY 182 north for 2.7 miles and turn left into the park.

Upland, ridge-top forest dominated by maple growing in shallow, limestone soils at the crest of the ridge at Carter Caves State Resort Park.

Civil War Earthen Works

Clark County Fiscal Court, Clark County, 25 acres

Defending the Kentucky River from Confederate raiders proved difficult for the Union Army. There were only two bridges across the river in Central Kentucky, yet there were at least 50 fords or ferries that allowed soldiers to cross easily. In 1863 there were a number of raids by Confederate Calvary that frustrated the Union Army, as the raiders created havoc by concealing their locations, crossing and re-crossing the Kentucky River, attacking isolated garrisons, and capturing and destroying Federal supplies.

The Union Army became increasingly frustrated and each time the Confederate Army came into the state, panic ran rampant. Captain Thomas B. Brooks, an engineer for the Central Kentucky region, had a solution and it was the same idea for protecting the L&N and Central Kentucky railroads. This idea was to create fortifications at the most important river crossings and three earthen work fortifications were created at Boonesboro, Clays Ferry, and Tate's Creek. The fortification at Boonesboro overlooked a ford in the bend (hence giving the town its name) and a ferry crossing at Boonesboro. African American Union soldiers built a square or rectangular fort that could be used to defend Kentucky River from the south or from attacks from the north.

What remains today are the eastern and western walls and trenches. The original road has been turned into trail that terminates at the top of the hill with a view overlooking the Kentucky River. The park consists of young calcareous forests dominated by sugar maple, and the open field at the top dominated by tall fescue and kept mown for visitors to see the earth works. The wooded section of the park is completely taken over by exotic, invasive plants that need to be removed to allow for more natural regeneration of the forest.

Access: Open dawn to dusk for hiking on a moderate to steep 1/2 mile trail with interpretative signs. From 1-64 take exit 94 and follow the bypass for 2.8 miles to KY Highway 627, Boonesboro Road. Follow 627 for 6.3 miles and turn right onto KY Highway 1924 and go 1.4 miles until you see the sign on the left side of the road and a mural painted on a concrete barrier. From 1-75 take exit 95 and go 6.1 miles to KY Highway 1924, then turn right and go 1.4 miles until you see the sign on your left. The trailhead begins at the parking lot.

Northern fence lizard on top of an old rock fence that overlooks the Kentucky River on the ridge crest at the Civil War Earthen works.

Clay Hill Memorial Forest

Campbellsville University, 100 of 250 total acres

Much of this tract was schedule to be logged and was purchased as an addition to Clay Hill Memorial Forest, which is a 158 research and educational forest and grassland that is owned and managed by Campbellsville University. This land was originally part of the Clay Hill Farm, which was one of largest plantations in Kentucky totaling over 4,000 acres. The woodland purchased by Kentucky Heritage Land Conservation Fund is a steep, forested ravine that leads down to Craig Creek. On the western side of the ravine the forest is dominated by tulip tree, sugar maple, red, black, white and chinquapin oak, shagbark hickory, American beech, American elm, and Ohio buckeye, and on the eastern side it is dominated by tulip tree and sassafras. Like much of Clay Hill Memorial Forest, the slopes provide habitat for a rich spring wildflower display including jack-in-the-pulpit, Jacob's ladder, Allegheny spurge, doll's eyes, bloodroot, trout lily, rue anemone, toothwort, and trilliums.

Access: Clay Hill Memorial forest has more than five miles of trails that are open to the public from dawn to dusk for passive recreation only. From the intersection of US-68/KY-55, turn right onto US-68 and proceed 1.1 miles to KY-289/Old Lebanon Avenue. Turn left on KY-298 and proceed for 8 miles. Clay Hill Memorial Forest is located on the right-hand side of the road.

Blue phlox and yellow trout lily decorate the forest floor near the stream at Clay Hill Memorial Forest.

Clay Wildlife Management Area

Kentucky Department of Fish and Wildlife Resources, Nicholas and Fleming Counties, 800 of 6,886 total acres

This wildlife management area is located in the outer Bluegrass Region characterized by rolling hills, with a mosaic of large grassland fields and smaller crop fields above mixed hardwood woodland and open ridge-top fields. It is approximately 85% forested and 15% open lands. Part of WMA borders Fleming Creek, which is a main tributary of the Licking River. There are two primary lower quality forest types, the calcareous mesophytic and sub-xeric calcareous forest. The sub-xeric forests occur near the ridge tops and are dominated by sugar maple, white ash, shagbark hickory, white, northern red, chinquapin, and black oaks with red maple, hackberry, blue ash, black cherry, tulip tree, black locust, and Ohio buckeye with an understory of bladdernut and plumleaf viburnum.

The mesophytic forests occur on lower slopes and are dominated by sugar maple, shellbark hickory, and Shumard oak with black maple, Ohio buckeye, black walnut, American elm, honey locust, and shagbark, bitternut, and shellbark hickories with and understory of spicebush and plumleaf viburnum. The riparian forest along Fleming Creek is dominated by boxelder, hackberry, honey locust with Ohio buckeye, American hornbeam, black walnut, sycamore, American elm, chinquapin oak, Black cherry, and bitternut and shellbark hickories. The forest has large amounts of invasive exotic plants including bush and Japanese honeysuckle, multiflora rose, privet, Garlic mustard, common chickweed, and Japanese stilt grass that can dominate the shrub and herbaceous layers. More than 143 species of plants, 71 birds, 27 mammals, 12 amphibians, and 9 reptiles have been observed.

Access: From Carlisle take KY 32 north and turn right on KY 3315 onto Cassidy Creek Road. There are two entrances and watch for signs. There are several boat ramps that provide access to the Licking River. Hunting and fishing are allowed following state seasons, except it is closed to the public during the quota fox hunting field trials. Open for passive and active recreation; no ATV are allowed.

Adult male white-tailed deer at the edge of the forest at Clay Wildlife Management Area.

Clear Creek Park Greenway

Shelby County Parks and Recreation Department 29 acres

Clear Creek Park is anchored by Lake Shelby on the north, which is a 20-acre fishing lake that was originally purchased in 1974 and was the city of Shelbyville's water supply. The park has a diversity of passive and active recreational opportunities and the land purchased by KHLCF protects a thin forest buffer along the creek. The land was purchased to add land to the greenway, which allows for expansion of trails, protect the undeveloped green space, and to provide access to creek for fishing, canoeing, wildlife viewing, and hiking, and environmental education.

The thin forest buffer is typical mesic and riparian forest and includes species such as black willow, box elder, silver maple, sycamore, pin and bur oak grading into more upland sites dominated by black walnut, shagbark and bitternut hickory, northern red oak, sugar maple, Ohio buckeye, American basswood, and blue and white ash. There are a few spring wildflowers that can be found including wood poppy, Dutchman's breeches, yellow trout lily, squirrel corn, spring beauty, and sessile trillium. Unfortunately, the exotic invasive garlic mustard has taken over much of the alluvial soils and is the dominant herbaceous plant, although river cane is rapidly expanding along the creek. Sixty-seven plant species and 133 bird species have been observed in the park.

Access: From US 60 in downtown Shelbyville turn north onto 7th Street and follow into Clear Creek Park onto Burks Branch Road.

Checkered white butterfly on common ironweed growing close to the creek at Clear Creek Park.

found include spiked lobelia, stiff gentian, smooth aster, several species of foxgloves and goldenrods. Rare species associated with this habitat include the state endangered ear leaf false foxglove, white rattlesnake root, starry false Solomon's seal, scarlet Indian paintbrush, rigid and cedar sedge and drooping bluegrass. State threatened species include the umbel-like sedge and slender blazingstar. State species of special concern include side-oats grama and Henslow's sparrow.

The forest surrounding the openings is semi-dry to dry calcareous type dominated by scarlet oak, pignut and shagbark hickory, sugar maple, black cherry, white ash, sassafras, red maple, and black gum with an understory of flowering dogwood, American hornbeam, and hophornbeam. The dry forests have gnarled and twisted post, chestnut, and blackjack oaks, red cedar, and sassafras with a sparse understory of blueberries. Some hayfields and old fields were originally seeded to tall fescue, orchard grass, timothy grass and sweet clover and some native species have invaded, particularly little bluestem, broomsedge, spiked blazing star, tall coreopsis, and gray-headed goldenrod. These fields have also become infested with Japanese honeysuckle, sweet clover, and Canada goldenrod.

Access: Due to the sensitivity of the site it is not open except by written permission only.

Indian paintbrush is one of the rare species found at Crooked Creek preserve. It is growing with Robin's plantain and eared coreopsis.

Crumps Cave Education and Research Preserve

Western Kentucky University, Warren County, 5 acres

This cave, historically known as Crump's, Cave Springs, Lisenby, or Smith's Grove Cave is 1.5 miles long and was a part of Cave Springs Farm Bed and Breakfast at the time Western Kentucky University purchased it. The purchase of the cave entrance, which was gated in 1994 to protect some ancient "mud glyphs" near the back of the cave from destruction, was to protect the cavern and sinkhole in addition to the mud glyphs. These Native American drawings are of geometric figures, animals and human figures in a clay wall dating back to 80 B.C.

One of the glyphs is an extremely rare representation of a human pregnant female, and it may be the oldest drawing of a female ever discovered in North America. During the archaeological inventory, another type of drawing, a charcoal drawing of an animal like a deer, was found near the entrance of the cave. Other important historical information suggests that the site was used as a hiding place for slaves along the "underground railroad", it served as Smith's Grove water supply, and the first 800 feet were used for cave tours by the bed and breakfast. Most of the remains of the water works have been removed from the cave and water quality research equipment has replaced it because Western Kentucky University now conducts unique research on water movement and quality in Karst systems in the cave.

Biologically, the cave serves as habitat for transient federally endangered gray bats in addition to big brown, little brown, and tri-colored bats, three cave beetles, a cave crayfish and a cave cricket. The uplands are primarily dominated by large chinquapin oaks, with an understory of wild hydrangea near the cave entrance.

Access: Open only by guided tour from Hoffman Environmental Research Institute at WKU due to sensitivity of the site.

A charcoal cave drawing of an animal on the wall by ancient people at Crumps Cave.

Cumberland Falls State Resort Park

Kentucky Department of Parks and Kentucky Division of Water Wild Rivers Program, McCreary County, 119 acres of 1,657 total acres

Called the "Niagara of the South", Cumberland Falls is most famous for its Moonbow, a faint rainbow that appears at the full moon under clear skies. Dr. Thomas Walker named the falls in 1750 after the Duke of Cumberland, the son of King George II of England. Hundreds of thousands of visitors have come from around the world to see this natural treasure.

The park was established in 1931 and grew from a few hundred acres to more than 1900 acres today. The first structures built were a cabin, which was followed by a small inn built in 1850 by Louis Renfro. This was later sold and renamed the "Moonbow Inn." The current lodge and cabins were built in the 1930's by the CCC, and the lodge was destroyed by fire and rebuilt in 1940. The additional acreage purchased by HLCF will serve as a buffer adjoining the river and the Daniel Boone National Forest.

The site is predominately ridgetop and upland dry forests dominated by chestnut, white, post, scarlet, black, and southern red oaks, and Virginia, pitch, and short leaf pine, red maple, mockernut hickory, and sourwood in the canopy and American chestnut, buffalo-nut, black huckleberry, box huckleberry, hillside blueberry, farkleberry, highbush blueberry, serviceberry, and mountain laurel in the understory. The mesic slope and ravine forests are dominated by hemlock, American beech, white, and northern red oak, red maple, cucumber tree, and tulip tree – some umbrella tree, big-leaf magnolia, sugar maple, bitternut hickory, pignut hickory, sweet gum, black cherry, basswood, and winged elm in the canopy. The understory is comprised of mountain camellia, mountain holly, American holly, redbud, and maple leaf viburnum.

There are several small wetland areas along the river that are dominated by ground cedar, cinnamon fern, royal fern, meadow selaginella, New York fern, and a variety of sedges and rushes. More than 155 plants species, 50 birds, 17 mammals, and 17 reptiles and amphibians have been documented. While no rare species were documented, the Allegheny wood rat, a federal spe-

Morning on the Cumberland River upstream from the falls where the HLCF property can be found on the opposite side of the river near this location.

cies of concern was observed in addition to some unusual Kentucky plants including hairy phlox, prairie heart-leaf aster, mountain Indian-physic, and mountain camellia. Six new prehistoric sites in rockshelters were also documented.

Access: This tract located to south and west of the Cumberland River Kentucky and Highway 90 via the Sheltowee Trace National Recreation Trail. This off trail area is not open to the public at this time without supervision from park personnel.

Luna moths are common on this preserve and can be seen roosting in the early morning during the spring months.

Davis Bend Watershed and Wildlife Conservation Area

Kentucky Division of Water Wild Rivers Program, Hart County, 166 acres

The Davis Bend Watershed and Wildlife Conservation Area is one of several sites KHLCF protects along the upper Green River. The state Wild Rivers Program purchased this one and one-half mile section of river frontage from the Kentucky Chapter of The Nature Conservancy, who retained the adjacent 110 acres of uplands with plans to develop an environmental education center. The outstanding scenic quality of this section of the Green River is a magical place called 300 Springs, and is best seen by visitors via paddling the river. Three separate 85' tall waterfalls that arise from springs drop over the top in the river.

The state threatened southern maidenhair-fern, which is often associated growing near waterfalls with travertine formations forms dense thickets around these falls. This section of the Green River is a globally recognized hotspot for mussel diversity. Populations of several federally endangered mussel species including the fanshell, northern rifleshell, ring pink, clubshell, rough pigtoe, catspaw, pink mucket, ring pink, and sheepnose. Federally endagered Indiana and gray bats also frequent this area.

Access: Due to limited access the site is not currently open to the public except by boat. Paddling access is available at Thelma Stovall Park in Munfordville; 300 Springs is approximate 15 river miles east of Munfordville.

One of three waterfalls found at Three Hundred Springs at Davis Bend on the Green River.

Dry Fork Gorge

Metcalfe County Fiscal Court, 80 acres

This gorge protects important karst topography and underground water resources and is the headwaters of the little Barren River, which drains into the Barren River and ultimately drains into the Green River. It lies within the boundaries of the International Bioreserve area of Mammoth Cave and four caves and seven springs are located in the gorge. Professionals from Mammoth Cave National Park indicate it has a very rich and diverse cave invertebrate fauna. It also has rich terrestrial forest habitats as more than 461 plant species observed, including many Appalachian species that are at the edge of their range.

Some of the forest is approaching old growth. Four distinct forest types have been observed including riparian forest, calcareous mesophytic forest, dry calcareous forest, and acid mesophytic forest. Uncommon to rare species include southern barrens lovegrass, noseburn, ginseng, western wood sorrel, and the state special concern white walnut. The riparian forest, streambank, and associated terrace communities are young and re-growing and are dominated by black walnut, tulip tree, box elder, sugar maple, and sweet buckeye. Because these areas were grazed or cut repeatedly in the past, it has a large amount of tree-of-heaven and weedy wildflowers such as peavine, harbinger of spring, white snakeroot, spreading waterleaf, Christmas fern, blue violet, and trilobed coneflower.

Calcareous mesophytic forest, which is much older and has fewer alien species, occurs on the lower slopes and benches. It is dominated by sugar maple with tulip tree, northern red oak, and white ash and an understory of wild hydrangea, paw paw, spicebush, bladdernut, hop hornbeam and leatherwood. This community type has a rich spring flower display including wild ginger, yellow trout lily, doll's eyes, spreading waterleaf, woodland phlox, foamflower, and large flowered trillium. Dry calcareous forest occurs on steep rocky slopes and is dominated by sugar maple, white and chinquapin oak, white ash, shagbark hickory with Shumard oak and bitternut hickory, slippery elm and blue ash as associates. Understory species include redbud, spicebush, hophornbeam, and coralberry with jack-in-the-pulpit, spring beauty, sessile trillium, shooting star, wild comfrey, yellow trout lily, and woodland phlox in the herbaceous layer. On the gentle upper slopes and ridges, large American beech and white oak with sugar maple, tulip tree and black oak dominate the acid mesophytic forest. Paw paw, hophornbeam and leatherwood are common understory species. Rockshelters protect habitat for the federally endangered gray bat.

Access: Two and a half mile unmarked foot trail open to hiking only. Hunting, fishing, camping and motorized, wheeled vehicles are not allowed. From Edmonton, take US 68/KY 80 west and turn left onto the Old Glasgow Rd. (Route 3234). Go up second hill past the S curve and turn left onto Branstetter Road. Go down Branstetter Road until you can no longer go straight and you will see the gate to the Gorge entrance right in front of you, follow the rock driveway up the hill and past the barn to the parking lot.

Large flowered white trillium and waterleaf near one of the forks of the streams in Dry Fork Gorge.

Eastview Barrens State Nature Preserve

Kentucky State Nature Preserves Commission, Hardin County, 120 acres co-owned with The Nature Conservancy

When the early settlers journeyed westward across Kentucky, they encountered large expanses of open fields or meadows that they called "The Big Barrens" region of Kentucky and Tennessee. This area was dominated by native grasses, particularly little bluestem, although other taller grasses such as Indiangrass and big bluestem occurred on deeper soils. Shrubs and stunted oaks and hickories were interspersed throughout and the native wildflowers were prolific in abundance. This system was maintained by fire, first by the Native Americans. The early settlers in the 1700's tended to avoid the barrens because of a lack of surface water from the karst topography and a lack of suitable timber for building. However, by the early to mid 1800's most of the barrens habitat was converted agriculture because of the fertile soils.

By the early 20th century, the Barrens were all but a memory and only small pockets, isolated fragments remain. If fire is not used to maintain the grasslands, forests will recover the land. One site that did escape was Eastview Barrens, because of the occasional fire set as sparks from a train on the adjacent railroad would ignite the dried grasses. This preserve protects one of best limestone and sandstone barrens complexes in the state. The showiest of the rare wildflowers found on the preserve is the state endangered prairie gentian. In addition, a very rare insect occurs here as well as the uncommon slender glass lizard. The vegetation is dominated by big bluestem, little bluestem, Indiangrass, poverty dropseed and the summer flowers are spectacular with rattlesnake master, blazingstars, evening primrose, Virginia lespedeza, sunflowers, bluehearts, goldenrods, goat's rue, St. John's worts, polygalas, wild quinine, angelica, wild petunia, pencil flower, trailing beans, and other species.

Access: No public access due to sensitivity of site but it is open by guided hike through the Kentucky State Nature Preserves Commission or Kentucky Nature Conservancy.

Rattlesnake master, sunflower, goldenrod, and other wildflowers in an area burned the previous spring at Eastview Barrens.

Flat Rock Glade State Nature Preserve

Kentucky State Nature Preserves Commission, Simpson County, 30 acres of 99 total acres

Flat rock cedar glades are among the rarest of all habitat types in the Southeastern United States. They are known primarily from the Nashville Basin area in Central Tennessee. Flat Rock Glade State Nature Preserve is the best example of a flat rock limestone cedar glade in Kentucky. The dominant feature of the glades, or forest openings, is large expanses of limestone bedrock that come to the surface and have thin gravelly soil in pockets where there is slight undulation in the rock and cracks and fissures. It is in these pockets of thin soil where you find a unique habitat that supports two state endangered plants, limestone fameflower and Butler's quillwort; state threatened plant species include upland privet, stemless evening primrose, eastern eulophus, hispid false mallow, and rough dropseed.

In the winter, these poorly drained areas are saturated with water and shooting star grows in abundance in the spring. The soils dry out in late spring and widows cross flowers profusely followed by prickly pear cactus. During the heat of the summer, the temperature on the exposed rock can exceed 125 F. Consequently the only type of vegetation found on the exposed rock is lichen and blue-green algae. The vegetation surrounding the five large open glades is a red cedar, chinquapin and post oak forest. As you move further from the exposed rock the forests transition to white-southern red-post oak forests or black and white oak forests. There is substantial red cedar, Carolina buckthorn and redbud trees that typically surround the open glades. For such a small area there is tremendous floristic diversity as over 102 plant species have been documented on the preserve.

Access: Not open to the public at this time due to the sensitivity of the site.

The largest glade opening at Flat Rock Glade State Nature Preserve with prickly pear cactus, widow's cross and fleabane.

Fort Heiman National Battlefield

Calloway County Fiscal Court transferred to the National Park Service, 167 acres

Ft. Heiman sits atop a high bluff overlooking Kentucky Lake and was one of three Civil War forts, Heiman, Henry and Donelson, built by the confederacy that provided protection for the Tennessee and Cumberland Rivers and a key rail line. It was named after Col. Adolphus Heiman of the 10th Tennessee Regiment, who commanded 1,100 troops at the fort and oversaw its construction, primarily by slaves in January 1862.

Union forces under U.S. Grant captured Fort Heiman just a month later in February 1862, and then captured Henry and finally Donelson 10 days later in February 1862. The fort was linear in shape on top of a bluff overlooking the river, and has two sets of remaining earthworks totaling 648 yards in length and between 8 to 10 feet deep. The Union forces remained at Fort Heiman for about a year. The importance of the site remained significant and in 1864, Confederate commander Nathan Bedford Forrest brought his cavalry and artillery and they shelled and sank several Union gunboats. He also boarded his men on a boat and raided Johnsonville, Tennessee, sinking ships and burning an important Union supply depot.

A coalition of various groups banded together to purchase dozens of subdivided parcels to protect the original fort site, and the land was handed over the National Park Service to become an installment of Fort Donelson National Battlefield. The land is mostly immature oak-hickory forest dominated by post and southern red oak and hickories, with white and scarlet oak, American beech, black gum and white ash as co-dominants.

Access: Open dawn to dusk for passive recreation only including hiking, biking, and running. No horseback or ATVs allowed. From Murray take KY highway 121 past New Concord to Cypress Trail on the left. Turn left and follow Cypress Trail until it intersects with Kline Trail, turn left and follow until it intersects with Fort Heiman Road and turn right until the road dead ends at the park and a one-way driving loop that overlooks Kentucky Lake.

View of sunrise over Kentucky Lake from the below the bluffs at Fort Heiman.

Frances Johnson Palk State Nature Preserve

Kentucky State Nature Preserves Commission, Pulaski County, 238 acres

This upland forest community is primarily Appalachian pine oak forest dominated by a mixture of shortleaf, pitch and Virginia pine with chestnut, scarlet, black, southern red, white and post oaks, and shellbark and mockernut hickories. Much of the forest is young and regenerating on the broad ridgetops. The midstory forest is dominated by mountain laurel, blueberries and huckleberries, black gum, sassafras and sourwood. The steep, mesic ravines are dominated by mixed hemlock forests that have a mixture of hemlock, American beech, white, and northern red oak, red maple, cucumber tree, and tulip tree. The most significant habitats on the preserve are the Appalachian acid seep communities that form at the head of several streams. These seeps are dominated by cinnamon and royal ferns, and more than 70 species of plants have been documented in them including the state threatened Eggert's sunflower and other rare plants, as well as one rare moth.

Access: No public access except with written permission or on guided field trips by Kentucky State Nature Preserves staff due to fragile resources and active resource management.

The white-fringeless or monkey faced orchid growing among cinnamon ferns in a seep at the Frances Johnson Palk State Nature Preserve.

Frenchman's Knob Conservation Area

Hart County Fiscal Court, 90 acres, written by Zeb Weese.

Frenchman's Knob supposedly was named for Gilbert LeClerc, who died on the top of the knob in 1788 after an Indian attack, which has been reported to be the last one in Kentucky. The historical society plans to restore a one-room schoolhouse found on the site. In addition to its historic significance, the area and adjoining property owned by the Southeastern Cave Conservancy, provides habitat for the federally endangered Indiana Bat and the once common Little Brown Bat, whose populations are declining because of White Nose Syndrome. Forest types are similar to other forests in the Knobs region and are dominated by oaks and hickories. The property will eventually be open to the public for hiking, bird watching and educational programs.

Access: From the Bonnieville exit on I-65, go East on KY 728 for a few yards then take the first right onto Frenchman's Knob Road. The site is 2.4 miles on the left; a gravel road leads up the hill to the trailhead parking, which is on the right side of the gravel road.

Redbuds and dogwoods show their colors at the edge of the forest in April.

Glenview Nature Preserve

Green County Fiscal Court, 76 acres

This county owned nature preserve protects more than one mile of Green River frontage, which is a global conservation priority because it is home to a rich and diverse aquatic fauna including 151 fish species, 71 mussels and numerous cave plants and animals. The upper Green is the main drainage in the central karst region, which is home to the world's largest cave system, Mammoth Cave and Kentucky's largest spring.

There are four distinct springs at Glenview and each one cascades down the rich wooded slopes to the Green River. Rare aquatic species found in the water include the federally endangered fanshell mussel, the state threatened rabbitsfoot mussel, and the state special concern stargazing minnow plus threadfoot, a state special concern plant that occurs in riffles in high quality aquatic systems. Other documented rare species include the state threatened nodding rattlesnake root, and state special concern spreading false foxglove and Henslow's sparrows.

Within the aquatic system there are a series of small scoured banks, riffles, and sand or gravel bars that are dominated by water willow, water-hemp, lowland thoroughwort, and marsh rice grass and the steep banks by the river are dominated by wild oats, wild rye grasses, and rice grass. This is a rich and diverse nature preserve, as more than 359 plant species have been observed. The riparian forest adjacent to the river contains much mature forest and large trees dominated by boxelder, silver maple, green ash, black walnut and hackberry.

There are large patches of paw paw and wild cane in the understory, as well as pea-vine, wild rye grasses, and wood nettle. The forest above the riparian zone on the terraces is dominated by American beech, Shumard oak, tulip tree, sweetgum, blackgum, white elm, bitternut hickory, shellbark hickory, and black walnut, which tend to dominate in some areas. The steeper lower moist forest above the terraces is mature and dominated by sugar maple, bitternut, and shagbark hickory, black walnut, hackberry, and northern red and chinquapin oak. Wild cane, hornbeam, hop-hornbeam, spicebush, bladdernut, and coral-berry dominate the shrub layer. The wildflowers are typical of previously grazed woodlands and are dominated by more weedy species although there are significant patches of nice spring wildflowers including wild hyacinth, bloodroot, squirrel corn, dwarf larkspur, blue phlox, shooting star, wild ginger, spring beauty, waterleaf, and Solomon's seal.

Access: Not open to the public at this time due to lack of vehicular access; a paddling trail is under development to allow access from the Green River by canoe or kayak.

Rue anemone growing near the stream at Baumgartner cascades which arises from a spring and flows into the Green River at Glenview Nature Preserve.

Green River State Forest

Kentucky Division of Forestry, Henderson County, 409 of 1,107 total acres

In response to the 1970's fuel crisis, the federal government purchased the original land in 1978 to build and develop a synthetic fuel research facility near the community of Henderson. The facility was never developed, and in 1998 the land was transferred to the Kentucky Division of Forestry as the Green River State Forest. The forest is a mixture of upland moist and dry forests, bottomland hardwoods, sloughs and wetlands, and reforestation sites. More than 538 acres of agricultural land have been planted and this is the site of Kentucky's first carbon sequestration project.

On the upland 400-acre forest there are ancient burial mounds that are archaeologically significant. These forests are dominated by white, post, southern red, bur, and shingle oak, red maple, shellbark, bitternut hickories, pecan, and catalpa on dry sites and American beech, tulip tree, sugar maple, black walnut, American elm, red elm, black and sweetgum, honeylocust, black cherry, American basswood, shagbark, pignut, and bitternut hickories,and northern red, overcup, swamp chestnut, pin, and cherrybark oak on moist sites. Moving downslope to the bottomlands, the forests are dominated by pin, cherrybark, overcup and willow oak, pecan, red maple, and sweetgum with bald cypress in the more permanently flooded areas.

Along the floodplain of the Ohio and Green Rivers, the sloughs are dominated by bald cypress, buttonbush, swamp holly, swamp privet and swamp mallow and the frequently flooded areas are dominated by silver maple, pin oak, cottonwood and swamp cottonwood, river birch and black willow. The riparian forests along the Ohio River are comprised of hackberry, sycamore, silver maple, green ash and American elm with a thick tangle of shrubs and vines including poison ivy, giant cane, trumpet creeper, grapes, porcelain berry, willows, elder berry and indigo bush. More than 189 species of plants, including the state threatened white nymph, have been observed in the forest. The bottomlands also provide habitat for the copperbelly water snake, a rare snake of this area.

Access: Open dawn to dusk by foot traffic only for hunting, fishing, hiking and other forms of passive recreation. ATV and off-road vehicles are prohibited and all state hunting and fishing regulations must be followed. Take US 60 east of Henderson approximately 3 miles to Tscharner Road and turn left, going north for approximately 1 mile and the forest will be on the left hand side of the road. Green River State Forest is very near the John James Audubon State Park.

Sunlight on the green ash trees in an old oxbow of the Green River on the Green River State Forest.

Griffith Woods

Kentucky Department of Fish and Wildlife Resources, Harrison County, 391 acres

When European settlers arrived in the Land of Cane and Clover throughout Central Kentucky, they were met by an unusual type of landscape in some areas dominated by a savanna-woodland complex where the forest canopy wasn't as dense and thick as they countryside they had been travelling through. While little to none of this ecosystem exists today because of human alteration of the habitat, particularly at the ground level, there are some patches of the old patriarch trees that dominate the skyline.

The Griffith farm has been in production agriculture for more than 200 years, and little of the native herbaceous or shrub layer exits because of cattle grazing and crop production; there is a 170 patch of remnant trees that is the best remaining example of Bluegrass savanna-woodland remaining in Kentucky. More than one half of the old, mature trees, ranging from 100 to 400 years old, are blue ash and another quarter of them are chinquapin oak. The national champion chinquapin oak can be found here and measures 76 feet tall, with a 69 foot spread and circumference of 311 inches. Other large trees include bur and Shumard oak, shagbark, shellbark, and bitternut hickory, Kentucky coffeetree, black maple, black walnut, and Ohio buckeye.

While most of the understory has been altered, there are still some scattered patches of pawpaw, American plum, American elderberry, Carolina buckthorn, wahoo, pasture rose, and various blackberries. Some herbaceous plants including various wild rye grasses and mayapple, sessile trillium, tall goldenrod, butterfly milkweed, wild hyacinth, yellow trout lily, and golden Alexander have been found in small numbers. Several hundred species of plants and at least 95 species of birds, 73 butterfly and moth species, 28 mammal species, and 13 species of reptiles and amphibians have been observed there. The one significant historical site located here is the old Griffith house, built around 1820 that served as an inn and tavern on the road from Lexington to Cincinnati in the 19th century.

Access: Not open to the public at this time, but it will be open as a wildlife management area when planning documents have been completed. Located at the corner of US Highway 62 and Kentucky Highway 353 with the entrance located approximately 1.4 mile from that intersection on US Highway 62.

Aerial shot of the savanna at Griffith Woods showing the widely spaced bur oak, blue ash, and hickory trees.

Gunpowder Creek, Boone Cliffs, and Dinsmore Woods

Boone County Fiscal Court, 299 acres

The purpose for protecting Upper Gunpowder Creek is to provide public accessibility for passive recreation and environmental education, and create a greenway with connectivity to a county nature preserve, a county park, a boy scout camp and a YMCA camp in Boone County. The Gunpowder Creek watershed encompasses more than 3,400 acres. This parcel lies in the northern reaches where urban and suburban development, along with de-icing chemicals from the Cincinnati-Northern Kentucky International Airport have severely impaired the water quality of the stream.

More than 50% of Boone county residents live within this watershed in one of the most rapidly developing counties in the state, and this nature preserve will be an important addition to the Boone County Parks. There is a 1.25-mile walking trail that leads from the parking area to the creek. While water quality is impaired, the surrounding forest is an excellent example of mature to old mixed, mesic bluegrass forest dominated by a variety of canopy species including white, red and blue ash; black cherry, white, chestnut, bur, and Shumard oak; tulip tree, big shellbark, shagbark and bitternut hickory; slippery and American elm; black and sugar maple, American beech; basswood; Kentucky coffeetree, and black walnut. Important understory species include sassafras, flowering dogwood, spicebush, redbud, pawpaw; bladdernut; yellow, sweet and Ohio buckeye; and American hornbeam.

As with most mesic bluegrass forest communities, this preserve has an outstanding spring wildflower display with typical limestone species occurring including synandra, doll's eyes, bloodroot, twinleaf, columbine, Goldenseal, several waterleaf, Jacob's ladder, spikenard, stonecrop, fire pink and wild ginger. The forest was in generally outstanding condition with few exotics until a tornado created several large canopy gaps which will allow for an increase in bush honeysuckle, garlic mustard, and other known invasive plant species. The bottomland forest communities adjacent to this excellent example of a braided stream include sycamore, black willow, American hop hornbeam, box elder, red maple; swamp white oak, pin oak, and buttonbush with an understory of a large number

Sycamores reflected in a pool at Gunpowder Creek.

of sedges, great blue lobelia, and swamp milkweed. More than 295 species of plants have been observed in the preserve. Thirty three birds, five mammals, three amphibians, and two reptile species have been observed on the preserve.

Access: Gunpowder Creek is open to the public from sunrise to sunset daily for passive recreation only. Parking is available at the north end by the picnic shelter prior to descending down the walking trail. The property is located at 6750 Sperti Lane, Burlington. From KY Route 18 (Burlington Pike) turn left onto East Bend Road at the four-way stop in Burlington. Go approximately 1 mile and turn left into Hanover Park subdivision onto Hanover Boulevard. Turn right onto Sperti Lane. The park is at the end of Sperti Lane on the left. Dinsmore Woods is located east of KY Route 18 approximately 10 miles west of Burlington, park on the west side of the road at Middle Creek Park. Boone Cliffs is about 1.5 miles from Dinsmore Woods near the end of Middle Creek Road on the left side.

Boone Cliffs and Dinsmore Woods are nearby sites that Boone County Fiscal Court also purchased using KHLCF funds to protect upland forests. They were both purchased from The Nature Conservancy and are also dedicated Kentucky State Nature Preserves. Dinsmore Woods is notably for its population of the federally endangered running buffalo-clover.

Squirrel corn is one of the many different species of wildflowers that occur at Boone Cliffs which is known for its excellent spring wildflower displays.

Dinsmore woods has a population of the federally endangered running buffalo clover and a small amount of old growth forest adjacent to the historic buildings.

Hawthorne Crossing Conservation Area

Campbell County Conservation District, 135 acres

The lower Licking River watershed is comprised of approximately 1.8 million acres and is home to more than 50 mussels, of which 11 are endangered and more than 70 species of fish including the highly prized muskie and paddlefish and the uncommon redside dace, mimic shiner, streamline chub, slender madtom, blue sucker, eastern sand, tippecanoe and sharpnose darters

The watershed is approximately 40% forested and 60% agricultural land, and the greatest threat to the system is excessive nutrient loads caused by agricultural fertilizer runoff, livestock manure, faulty septic and sewer systems, and non-point source pollution. This conservation area protects 3,000 linear feet of riverbank and associated riparian forest, and more than 2,000 linear feet of riffle creek, including the confluence with the Licking River.

In 2012, an extensive stream and wetland restoration project was completed by the Northern Kentucky University's Center for Applied Ecology. The forested habitats are mostly young and regenerating, with poor species diversity and have been heavily invaded with non-native invasive plants, particularly bush honeysuckle. The riparian forest is dominated by small silver maple and box elder trees with the occasional sycamore, cottonwood, osage orange, black walnut, slippery elm and hackberry. The herb layer in places contains a good diversity of native plants including various wild rye grasses, phlox, dwarf larkspur, wingstem, white snakeroot, violets, bedstraw, wild bean, common groundsel, wild ginger, waterleaf, corn salad, and goldenglow and in other areas is completely dominated by exotics including Japanese grass, Japanese hops, garlic mustard winter creeper, and reed canary grass.

The upland forests are also young and dominated by red cedar, osage orange, honey locust and black locust with an understory of bush honeysuckle. Other trees occasionally found in the forests include scarlet and chinquapin oak, white ash, sugar maple, pignut hickory, Ohio buckeye, black walnut and slippery elm. The remaining 12% of the land is overgrown old fields, pastures, and shrub thickets dominated by tall goldenrod, tall fescue, smooth brome, orchard grass, and a wide variety of invasive exotic plants including multiflora rose, Queen Anne's lace, spotted knapweed, garlic mustard, teasel, red and white clovers, bush honeysuckle and osage orange. There is one small wet meadow dominated by sedges, rushes, swamp milkweed, agrimony, and bugleweed. One hundred forty four plant species have been documented on the property of which 21% are exotic, invasive species.

Access: Not open to the public at this time until a management plan has been approved and trails have been constructed.

Carolina Chickadees are common residents seen perching on young trees in the Hawthorne Crossing Conservation Area.

Hazeldell Meadow

Pulaski County Fiscal Court, 39 acres

This unique flatwoods and highland rim wet barrens or prairie is a tiny remnant of this globally rare plant community type, purchased from the Nature Conservancy. Most of the preserve is underlain by a sandy fragipan soil, which means that it has seasonally standing water in both the wooded and open habitats. The best example of this plant community type remaining is May Prairie in Central Tennessee, and this preserve protects a tiny amount of the biodiversity of what historically occurred in this habitat type. The small opening, less than 2-acres in size, is dominated by various grasses, sedges and rushes including velvet witchgrass, arctic reedgrass, broomsedge, and bushy broomsedge and is the only known Kentucky location for the state endangered shortleaf skeleton grass. Other rare plants found here include the only known location for the state endangered dwarf or red sundew and state endangered hairy water primrose, narrow-leafed sundrops, and southern club moss; state threatened St. Andrew's cross, and state special concern round-headed bush clover and globe beaked rush. Most of the preserve is seasonally wet flatwoods dominated by red maple, sweet gum, black gum, American beech, white oak, pin oak, scarlet oak, and American holly.

Access: Open to public foot traffic on established trails. From Kentucky Highway 39, turn east onto Ocala Road and follow it for 1.4 miles and look for Hazeldell Church on the right hand side of the road. There is a gravel parking lot to the left of the church.

Yellow fringed orchids can be found in abundance at this site along with numerous rare plants including sundews.

Hi Lewis Pine Barrens State Nature Preserve

Kentucky State Nature Preserves Commission, Harlan County, 302 acres

Rising over 1,000 feet from the southern base to the ridge of Pine Mountain, this preserve, purchased in part from the Nature Conservancy, protects the best known example of an open pine-woodland ecosystem dominated by pitch and short-leaf pine and chestnut oak. The understory has numerous drought tolerant species including blueberries and mountain laurel with little bluestem and Indiangrass as dominant herbaceous species. Bracken fern is also abundant, and other dominant forbs found in the community include galax, narrowleaf silkgrass, trailing arbutus, goat's rue, false foxglove, French grass, naked tick trefoil, whorled loosestrife, Maryland golden aster, and goldenrods.

This site protects the only known populations of state endangered Canada Frostweed and populations of state threatened yellow screwstem and the largest population of state threatened yellow wild indigo in state. There are also fruit producing American chestnut trees at this site and overall more than 94 plant species plants, 32 liverworts, 89 mosses 7 amphibians, 8 reptiles, 16 mammals, 61 insects have been documented including two rare bats, the Indiana and small footed myotis, and one rare insect. In the open areas under a powerline, a more representative Pine Barrens type community can be seen and uncommon species like butterfly pea can also found. The other open areas consist of large sandstone outcrops, where you find stunted pines and scarlet and chestnut oaks with some winged sumac and a ground cover that is mostly bare rock but interspersed with some little bluestem, narrow leaf silkgrass, Indiangrass and bracken fern.

Seven ecological communities occur in this small preserve, but the most significant is the Appalachian xeric pine savanna-woodland, which has a sparse canopy and prairie like understory. This

Small opening surrounded by mountain laurel, yellow pine, and sourwood at Hi Lewis Pine Barrens State Nature Preserve.

globally imperiled community was historically maintained by fire and the area was burned a dozen times in the 20th Century. Recent disturbance after the 2000 fire in the sub-xeric forest, pine-oak forest and Appalachian mesophytic forest have given rise to shrubs and thickets of red maple, sassafras, American chestnut, blackberries, greenbrier and in less disturbed sites some canopy species including black oak, scarlet oak, chestnut oak with pignut hickory and white oak remain.

In the mesic sites the forest is young and dominated by tulip tree, white and northern red oak, sweet birch, cucumber tree and in hemlock dominated forests near the bottom you find eastern hemlock, tulip tree, northern red oak and sweet birch with mid-story of Frasier's magnolia, great laurel, and wild hydrangea. In addition to the fire, southern pine beetle destroyed many of the pines and are being replaced by thickets of red maple, sassafras and young pines and providing intense competition for resources resulting in a reduced herbaceous community in these areas.

Access: No public access except with written permission or on guided field trips by KSNPC staff due to fragile resources and active resource management. Located off the Little Shepherd Trail.

Canada Frostweed is only known to occur at Hi Lewis Pine Barrens in Kentucky and several other locations on Pine Mountain.

Hidden River Cave

City of Horse Cave, Hart County, 10 acres in three tracts

This cave is part of a large karst system that drains 100 square miles in West-Central Kentucky and is connected to Mammoth Cave, the largest cave system in the world with over 350 miles of underground passages. The entrance, located in downtown Horse Cave, is a large sinkhole and the water in the cave flows under the city of Horse Cave and re-emerges along the Green River as springs of which five of the largest springs in Kentucky are associated with this karst system in Hart County. It originally opened as Horse Cave around the turn of the century. Tours were routinely given from 1927 until 1943.

This cave was once known as the most polluted cave in North America due to industrial and domestic waste issues, and it was closed from 1943 until 1993 when a new waste treatment facility began treating those problems. This is significant because the water from the cave system enters the Green River, which is one of the most important freshwater streams left in North America and supports more than 70 mussel species of which 17 are rare and one is the only Kentucky endemic, 150 species of fish of which 13 are rare including 7 endemics, the federally endangered KY cave shrimp, the endemic bottlebrush crayfish, and numerous other rare organisms.

The cave itself has no spectacular formations, but does provide habitat for unique cave critters including the state special concern southern cavefish and eyeless crayfish, two trogolbitic invertebrates including an isopod and amphipod, and a copepod which is only known from one other location. The purpose of protecting this land was to protect and manage Hidden River Cave and to work with the American Cave Conservation Association to provide an example of how to protect an underground cave and watershed from the threats of inadequate sewage treatment, contaminants from traffic and businesses, spills from trains, intrusions of oil and gas drilling and pollution from agricultural runoff. The ultimate goal is to develop an education program in coordination with the American Cave Conservation Association.

Access: Open to the public via guided programs on elevated trails above floor of cave passages to avoid sensitive habitats. Located 2.2 miles east of I-65 at Exit 58. Take State Highway 218, cross the railroad tracks and pass the stoplight (intersection of 218 & 31W). The American Cave Museum and Hidden River Cave are on the right. Parking is available curbside.

The entrance of hidden river cave located in downtown Horse Cave.

High View Hill

Ohio County Fiscal Court, 257 acres

This park is a mixture of young regenerating forest 10 to 20 years old and older more mature forest, old fields reverting to forest, old abandoned strip mine, and riparian forest along the Green River. There are also rocky outcroppings and a cave on the slope overlooking the river. The more mesic slope forests are dominated by sugar maple and the ravines are dominated by American beech, whereas the upland forests are dominated by oaks, primarily white and chestnut. The understory is a mixture of paw paw, spicebush, greenbrier, Christmas fern, and various grasses. The old fields reverting back to forest have much tulip tree, black walnut, sweet gum, white ash, and sassafras. There is typical riparian forest along the river dominated by silver maple, box elder, and sycamore with some Shumard oak and sugarberry and an understory of various sedges and Virginia wild rye. There is a significant problem with invasive species here with large amounts of tree-of-heaven and red mulberry along all the forest edges. At least 62 plant species have been observed at this site.

Access: Open dawn to dusk daily for passive recreation only. No mountain bikes, off-road vehicles, ATV's or horses are allowed on the trails. From the Beaver Dam exit on the West Kentucky Parkway, travel south on US 231 and take the first right onto KY 269. Follow KY 269 south past Prentiss to Barnes Lane and turn left and follow until you see the park entrance on the left and if you continue the road turns into overlook river road and there is a public boat ramp to access the Green River at the bottom of the hill.

View of the Green River early in the morning from atop a bluff at High View Hill Park.

James E. Bickford State Nature Preserve

Pine Mountain Settlement School and Kentucky State Nature Preserves Commission, Harlan County, private nature preserve dedication of 348 acres of the school's 623 total acres

Founded in 1913 as a boarding school for the elementary and middle school children of the southeastern Kentucky mountains, Pine Mountain Settlement School has a mission of providing environmental education and traditional arts and culture to more than 3,000 participants annually. Listed on the National Register of Historic Places, the nature preserve component of the school protects a high quality Appalachian mesic forest on the north slope of Pine Mountain, and protects numerous rare species including state endangered fetterbush, state threatened American golden saxifrage, Loesel's twayblade, and state special concern rock harlequin in addition to the state special concern Masked shrew.

In addition, several endemic cave invertebrates including Roger's cave beetle, scholarly cave beetle, and un-described cave-obligate freshwater isopod and un-described cave-obligate millipede are also found here. As with typical Appalachian mixed-mesophytic forest, no one tree species dominates the canopy and 27 tree species have been found in canopy, including many mature and large trees. There are three species achieving some dominance and those are tulip tree, sugar maple, and American basswood, with bitternut hickory, yellow buckeye, and cucumber magnolia following close behind.

The other two forest communities found here include the mixed hemlock stands dominated by eastern hemlock, American beech, tulip tree and yellow birch with an understory of Frasier's magnolia, big-leaf magnolia and great rhododendron. The ridge-top forests are dominated by chestnut oak with red maple, black gum and pignut hickory with midstory of eastern hop hornbeam, red maple, maple leaf viburnum, and mountain laurel. It has changed greatly as fire and the American chestnut have disappeared from the landscape.

More than 615 species of plants have been documented here and the spring wildflower display is diverse as more than 130 spring wildflowers including wood poppies, dwarf larkspur, spotted and yellow mandarin, large flowered trillium and purple wake robins, large flowered bellwort, wild geranium, bloodroot, dwarf crested iris, and speckled wood lily occur in abundance. The area was named in honor of James Bickford, former Secretary of the Kentucky Cabinet for Natural Resources.

Access: Open to the public during approved environmental educational programs such as the wildflower weekends or Lucy Braun workshops or by making provisions with the director. If you are coming from the northwest or north along the I-75 corridor, you can take exit 29 (Corbin US 25E) to Pineville. Take a left at the second stoplight (KY 66/221) and follow this road for 1.5 miles (going east). At this junction turn right onto 221 and go 24 miles to the intersection of US 421 and veer to the left (this intersection is on a curve) to stay on 421/221 and in 0.9 miles take a hard right to continue onto 221. Follow this for another 10 miles until you reach the junction of 221 and 510 and veer to the right on 510, then take an immediate right into the Settlement School.

Catawba rhododendron in flower at the top of the Bickford State Nature Preserve along the Little Shepherd Trail.

JEFFERSON MEMORIAL FOREST

Metro Parks, City of Louisville, Jefferson and Bullitt County, 621 of 6,248 total acres in six tracts

This is one of the nation's largest urban forests started in 1945 when 1300 acres were acquired by 1948. More land was added during several distinct periods of recent history during the environmental awakening period in the 60's and 70's, in the early 80's and late 80's, and most recently in the 90's until today with assistance from Kentucky Heritage Land Conservation Fund funds.

The forest serves as a recreational Mecca for the citizens of Jefferson County and the Commonwealth in general, with over 35 miles of hiking trails, horseback riding trails, playgrounds and pavilions, fishing, tent camping, and as a resource for environmental education. The forest is generally grouped into three categories: the recreational forest (26%), which is generally considered to be poor in quality with associated lawns, meadows and other open areas, the recovering forest (40%) which is an area of better quality forest that will be allowed to recover from past disturbances, and the significant resource area (34%), which is the highest quality forest that will be restored to mature status.

The forest community found on lower slopes and ravines is the acidic mesophtyic dominated by American beech, sugar maple, white and northern red oak, and tulip tree with understory of flowering dogwood, pawpaw, maple leaf viburnum, spicebush, hornbeam, ironwood, and hearts-a-burstin'. On the north and east slopes of this community you will find rich spring wildflower displays of wild ginger, baneberry, jack-in-the-pulpit, blue cohosh, twinleaf, Solomon's seal, waterleaf, and other species. On the upper slopes and ridges the forest changes to a drier acidic forest dominated by white, black, chestnut oak, southern red, and scarlet oak; pignut, mockernut and sweet pignut hickory; with sourwood, mountain laurel, and low bush blueberry in the understory.

Contained within this forest in small narrow bands is a more open type of forest with an open canopy and widely spaced post, blackjack, and chestnut oaks, with some highbush and low bush blueberries in the understory. The highest and driest forest found here is a pine-oak forest dominated by Virginia Pine and chestnut, scarlet and black oak. One unique community found here is the shale barren, which is an area of exposed bedrock and shallow soils with sparse vegetation except a few chestnut and post oaks with some native grasses, rough blazing star, bird-foot violet and hairy wood mint. More than 283 plant species, including the state endangered narrow-leaf bluecurls and rare little ladies tresses have been observed. More than 32 amphibians, 135 birds, 37 reptiles, and 34 mammals have been found here.

Access: Open 8:00 am to dusk except Dec 24 and 25 and Jan. 1 for hiking, fishing (Tom Wallace Lake), tent camping, horse-

A night time view of the airport and downtown Louisville from the top of a knob at Jefferson Memorial Forest.

back trails, picnic shelters and playgrounds, and environmental education including camps. To get there from I-65 take I-265 West (Gene Snyder Freeway) to the New Cut Road exit and turn left, going south. Travel approximately 1.2 miles and at the yellow flashing light, turn right onto Mitchell Hill Road. Travel 1.5 miles and turn left into the Welcome Center parking lot (11311 Mitchell Hill Road). The Welcome Center is a white, two-story building with a red roof.

Red maples turning color along with red cedar in the understory growing at the edge of the Jefferson Memorial Forest.

Jessamine Creek Nature Preserve

Jessamine County Fiscal Court, 269 acres

This nature preserve is one of the "gems" of the palisades region of the Kentucky River and was purchased from the Nature Conservancy. The site contains more than 560 species of plants including seven rare species, caves that are home to two different federally endangered bat species, multiple springs feeding into a beautiful stream, a 60' tall waterfall, and forests that support a rich spring wildflower display. The narrow and steep slopes of the gorge and associated cliffs gives rise to forest communities ranging from alluvial stream floodplain forests dominated by sycamore, box elder and silver maple, to very dry narrow rocky ridges or "points" where many of the rare species including cleft phlox, mountain lover, Walter's violet, and purple oatgrass occur.

Other rare species known include Downy and soft-leaf arrowwood, water stitchwort and snow trillium. The moist slope forest communities are dominated by sugar maple and northern red oak with white and chinquapin oak, basswood, white ash, and Ohio buckeye. Smaller trees include bladdernut, flowering dogwood, and American hop hornbeam. This plant community has a rich spring wildflower display with bloodroot, twinleaf, hepatica, purple phacelia, sessile trillium, rue and false rue anemone, wild ginger and many other species. Moving upslope to the drier habitats, the forest community changes composition and chinquapin oak and blue ash dominate with red cedar and rock elm becoming common. Understory species include redbud, Carolina buckthorn, and vibrunums. The upland flat ridge tops and blufftops are dominated by a variety of oaks including white, post, shingle, and black and shagbark, pignut and mockernut hickories.

Access: Public access is limited to special guided hikes offered by the Jessamine County Fiscal Court.

Snow trillium only occurs in several places in central Kentucky in forested gorges along the palisades and the largest population occurs at the Jessamine Creek Nature Preserve.

Jim Scudder State Nature Preserve

Kentucky State Nature Preserves Commission, Hardin County, 172 of 230 total acres in two tracts

This nature preserve protects one of best limestone slope glade complexes in the state. At least five major dry, rocky openings provide habitat for prairie species like the state endangered Barrens silky aster, and state special concern Crawe's sedge. More than 279 plant species have been documented from the property.

The most significant habitat located in the dry, rocky openings is the limestone slope glade, which occurs on south and southwest facing slopes and is dominated by drought tolerant grasses including poverty dropseed, Indiangrass, and little bluestem with big bluestem in deeper soils. These openings also have rich wildflower displays of hoary puccoon, prairie phlox, columbine, wavy leaf and pale purple coneflower, pale spiked lobelia, wild bergamot, gray headed coneflower, roundseed St. John's wort, black-eyed susan, butterfly milkweed, false aloe, several blazingstars, sunflowers, silphiums, and goldenrods. Surrounding the glades is a semi-open dry woodland habitat dominated by red cedar and chinquapin oak with Eastern redbud in the understory.

The herb layer is similar to what is found in the openings. Scorpions and fence lizards are common inhabitants of these dry, rocky habitats. On exposed limestone ridges you find dry calcareous forest or woodland with blue ash, bur oak, red cedar, and chinquapin oak dominating the canopy. Most of the preserve is forested and dominated by calcareous sub-xeric forests of white oak, pignut hickory, white ash, northern red oak and shagbark hickory with an understory of sugar maple, black gum, and hop hornbeam. The richest forest type, calcareous mesophytic forest, occurs on the slopes and stream bottoms with a canopy of black walnut and Ohio buckeye. Common midstory species include blue beech, flowering dogwood, and wild hydrangea with a rich spring wildflower display of wild geranium, wild ginger, blue phlox, sessile trillium, green dragon, spring beauty, dwarf larkspur, Dutchman's breeches, twin leaf, and Solomon's seal. More than 46 birds including some declining neotropical species like ovenbirds, Kentucky warbler, and red eyed vireo, have been documented in addition to seven mammals, eight amphibians, five reptiles, and 22 butterflies.

Access: No public access except with written permission or on guided field trips by KSNPC staff due to fragile resources and active resource management. Located off Springfield Road, Elizabethtown.

Prairie phlox flowering in early spring at Jim Scudder State Nature Preserve.

JULIAN SAVANNA

Kentucky State Nature Preserves Commission, Franklin County, 42 acres conservation easement

The bluegrass savanna woodland complex is a globally rare community type that is unique to the Central Kentucky Bluegrass Region. This community type has largely become extinct, although a few remnant sites with trees that are more than 200 years old can still be found. This particular patch of degraded bluegrass savanna woodland complex has numerous over 4' diameter chinquapin and white oaks and blue ash.

The site is highly degraded from over-grazing use as a pasture and dominated by tall fescue and bluegrass. Numerous invasive exotic plants including garlic mustard, musk thistle, poison hemlock, crown vetch, Queen Anne's lace, autumn olive, bush and Japanese honeysuckle, stilt grass, and multiflora rose contribute to the degradation as a natural community. The property has been in the Julian family since 1812 and was grazed by cattle and sheep, but the ground was never plowed or fertilized.

Grazing ceased in 1993 and site has been burned resulting in some shrubs invading including box elder, coral berry, blackberry, and rough leaf dogwood. On one corner of the property there is a young calcareous mesophytic forest with box elder, black walnut and black cherry in the canopy and some native herbs, wood mint, cut-leaf toothwort, Virginia wildrye, bergamot, Miami mist, mayapple and sessile trillium, in the herbaceous layer. There is also an old field thicket of invasive exotic shrubs and fescue at the other end of the preserve. The goal of this property is to restore the savanna community.

Access: Due to site sensitivity and private ownership, this preserve is not open to the public.

Sunset over a large blue ash at the Julian savanna.

Kentenia State Forest

Kentucky Division of Forestry, Harlan County, 762 of 4,277 total acres in four tracts

This is the first state forest in Kentucky and was dedicated in 1919 when Kentenia-Cantron Corporation donated the land to the state. Sitting on top and the south face of Pine Mountain, this forest is mostly dry Appalachian forest with mixed hemlock stands in the ravines and drainages. It is mostly flat on top with numerous large rock outcroppings and some cliffline and rockhouse habitat but then drops into steep slopes dominated by Chestnut, scarlet, southern red, and white oaks, red maple, black gum, sweet birch and Virginia and pitch pines.

As you move down the slopes, the forest changes in composition with red and sugar maple, northern red and chestnut oak, tulip tree, black gum, black locust, Fraser's magnolia, cucumber tree, eastern hemlock and pines dominating. The lower slopes are dominated by the same species except white oak becomes a significant component of the canopy. The ravines and drainages are mixed hemlock stands with eastern hemlock, tulip tree, and sugar maple in the canopy and large stands of great rhododendron.

The cliffline and rockhouses are dominated by various lichens, mosses, ferns, round-leaf catchfly, pink lady slipper, and rockhouse alumroot. More than 250 species of plants have been documented in the forest and include the following rare species: state threatened yellow wild indigo, small yellow lady slipper, Steele's joe-pye-weed, Curtis' goldenrod; state endangered American chestnut and state special concern small enchanter's nightshade, spinulose wood fern, showy gentian and white walnut.

Access: Open to the public for hiking, nature study, hunting, fishing, horseback riding and primitive camping. Off-road vehicles are not permitted. Parking is limited to various locations at pullouts along the Little Shepherd Trail. From Harlan, take US 119 east to the junction of US 421 and turn north proceeding up the mountain until you reach the Little Shepherd Trail; this section of the Little Shepard is part of the Pine Mountain Scenic Trail. Turn right onto the gravel road and the state forest is located along the road on the south side.

Forest canopy in fall color at Kentenia State Forest from overlook on Kentucky Highway 2010.

Early morning fog in Sand Pond, a popular spot in Kentenia State Forest.

Kentucky Ridge State Forest and Wildlife Management Area

Kentucky Department of Fish and Wildlife Resources and Kentucky Division of Forestry, Bell County, 3,782 of 15,251 total acres

Sitting above the community of Pineville and lying immediately adjacent to Pine Mountain State Park and Kentucky Ridge State Forest, this wildlife management area consists of forested habitat on the north slope of Pine Mountain and the Cumberland Plateau. The portion of the management area on the plateau has an extensive history of deep and strip mining going back to the early 1900's and as recently as 1986. Consequently this particular forest has been heavily impacted by man and disturbance.

It is rough terrain with vegetation dominated primarily by invasive exotic species such as multiflora rose, autumn olive, princess tree and early successional native species such as black and honey locust and red maple. Other forms of disturbance including at least three rounds of logging, southern pine beetles, and frequent fire. The loss of American chestnut and invasive exotic plants have dramatically altered the plant communities. The best forested communities occur where logging has been the only disturbance on Pine Mountain, and those are typically mixed mesophtyic forests dominated by younger trees of sugar maple, yellow buckeye, white basswood, tulip tree, cucumber tree, northern red oak, and bitternut hickory. The lower slopes are dominated by white oak, American beech, and sugar maple, whereas the upper slopes are more mixed oak stands with white, chestnut, scarlet, black, and northern red oaks dominating with some American beech. Sites above the strip mines are typically dominated by red maple, white oak, and tulip tree. A total of 314 plant species have been documented as well as 19 amphibian, 14 reptile, 13 mammal, and 123 bird species.

Access: Open to the public daily according to statewide wildlife management area regulations. Public hunting is available under statewide regulations for all hunting and trapping seasons and open for passive and active recreation including primitive camping, hiking, and picnicking. ATVs are not allowed. From Pineville go north on US 25E to the intersection with Kentucky Highway 92 and turn west (left), then travel four miles. Look for the parking area with signage on the left.

Long leaf rhododendron in the early morning fog in a rich cove site at Kentucky Ridge State Forest and Wildlife Management Area.

Kentucky River Wildlife Management Area

Kentucky Department Fish and Wildlife Resources, Owen and Henry County, 534 of 2,620 total acres in two tracts

This management area is bordered by the Kentucky River and is reverting farmland, pastures, and woodland. The total property is 76% forested and 22% open land, with wetland making up the remaining habitat types. The land purchased with Kentucky Heritage Land Conservation funds is approximately 28% forested with riparian forest and bottomland hardwood forest in the low lying areas and calcareous mesophytic forest on the uplands. There is one open marsh dominated by marsh cut grass, common rush, Carolina willow and Uruguayan water primrose.

The Riparian forests are dominated by silver maple, black walnut, sycamore, box elder, hydrangea and coralberry, marsh blue violet, stinging nettle, stream bank wild rye, wild oats, poison ivy, and hog peanut. The bottomland forest is made up of American elm, box elder, sliver maple and lizard tail which is somewhat rare in the Bluegrass Region. The upland calcareous forests are dominated by sugar maple, yellow oak, mockernut hickory, and northern hackberry. The understory has been heavily grazed and is dominated by exotic organisms including garlic mustard, henbit and chickweed. The woodlands have been invaded by bush honeysuckle, Japanese honeysuckle, privet, and Japanese stilt grass.

The open fields are reverting agricultural land and poison hemlock, nodding thistle, bull thistle, amaranth, burdock, fescue and johnson grass and Japanese hops are some of the dominant species. No rare species have been found although northern leopard frogs, which are uncommon, have been found breeding here. More than 226 plant species, 40 fish, 88 birds, 12 mammals, 17 amphibians, and 12 reptiles have been documented on this management area. The Department of Fish and Wildlife Resources is working on converting the old fescue fields to native warm season grasses and expanding the riparian forests by planting trees. Several sunflower fields are located on the area to promote dove hunting.

Access: Open to the public daily according to statewide wildlife management area regulations. Public hunting is available under statewide regulations for all hunting and trapping seasons, except no firearms are permitted for deer hunting. To get to the Welch bottomland tract that is disabled accessible, travel one mile southwest of Gest on KY 561. Look for the parking area on the east side of the road. To get to the Owen county tract, go one mile south of Gratz on Brown's Bottom Road and look for the parking area on the left side of the road.

Sunflower field for dove hunting at the Kentucky River Wildlife Management Area.

Tom wild turkeys in a grassy opening adjacent to the forest.

Kentucky State University Environmental Education and Research Center

Henry County, 305 acres

The environmental education center was originally created by the Kentucky School for the Blind to create a center where the environment could be accessible to students regardless of physical limitations. Kentucky State University has worked to keep this dream alive by working with various collaborators to make this learning facility disabled accessible by putting in paved trails with educational overlooks and a disabled accessible bird blind, pavilion, and two-tiered platform that overlooks a one-acre pond.

The site was originally a farm and is now reverting back to forest with oak-hickory forests covering 49% of the land base. These forests are dominated by bur, Shumard, and chinquapin oaks, shellbark and bitternut hickory, black walnut, and Ohio buckeye. Red cedar transitional forests occur on 27% of the land base and these habitats are dominated by red cedar but have much Shumard and chinquapin oak, shagbark and pignut hickories, white ash, slippery elm, and sugar maple coming up in the understory. The calcareous mesic forests are dominated by sugar maple, northern red oak, tulip tree and chinquapin oak.

Forests along six mile creek, which runs through the property, are dominated by sycamore, green ash, silver maple, box elder and American hornbeam. More than 245 plant species have been recorded from the property. There is a population of the state threatened green false hellebore, state special concern, nodding rattlesnake root, and populations of several uncommon plants including limestone calamint, ginseng, and Missouri river willow. Since the center has opened, thousands of visitors ranging from school children to university graduate students have visited the preserve.

The center promotes active research projects and several include genetic analysis of native paw paw trees, how exotic or native plants affect leaf beetle diversity and how various trail surfaces affect disabled access with the National Center for Accessibility. The center cooperates with a variety of entities including the KY Readymix Association, Xerox, Home Depot, Shooting Star Nursery, and others to develop the site to meet their goal of making every reasonable effort to provide access to all members of the Commonwealth while focusing on providing educational experiences that accommodate different learning abilities. KSU received the 2009 KHLCF Stewardship Award for their management efforts.

Access: From Frankfort, visitors should travel 12.5 miles north on U.S Highway 421. North of mile marker 17 visitors should turn east onto Little Dixie Road. Travel 2.6 miles on Little Dixie Road and the front gate to the Environmental Education and Research Center will be on the left. The center is open dawn to dusk for hiking and other outdoor recreational activities by contacting the manager. Overnight camping is allowed with two weeks notice. No firearms or vehicular travel is allowed on the property.

Duckweed on farm pond with sugar maple forest at the Kentucky State University Environmental Education and Research Center

Tremendous efforts have been made to add infrastructure to this center to facilitate use by disabled individuals; photo by Joe Dietz.

Knobs State Forest

Kentucky Division of Forestry, Bullitt County, 1,539 acres

This former tree farm was the first Forestry Legacy project in Kentucky; 96% of the land is forested with the remaining acreage seeded to native warm season grass fields. The forest is an important link in creating a contiguous large forest block that includes Bernheim Forest, the Crooked Creek Boy Scout Reservation, and the Fort Knox military installation.

This particular forest tract has a long history of logging dating back to the mid 1840's, when the forest was rapidly cleared to feed an iron furnace in the 1840's. It was then selected logged in the 1980's, and in the 1990's some tracts were clear cut and at the present time white oak and chestnut oak account for 60% of the tree canopy.

The primary forest types found at the forest include a Virginia Pine forest dominated by the pine and black, scarlet, and chestnut oak, red cedar, and pignut hickory with an understory of blueberry and greenbrier. The upper slopes are acidic sub-xeric forests with a canopy of chestnut, scarlet, black, and post oak, shagbark and mockernut hickory, red maple, black gum, and winged elm, with an understory of flowering dogwood, sassafras, redbud, red cedar, Carolina buckthorn, coralberry, downy serviceberry, blueberry, and greenbrier.

The slope and ravine forests are acidic mesophytic with a canopy of American beech, white and northern red oak, sugar maple, black cherry, red maple, tulip tree, and sweet gum with an understory of slippery elm, black gum, sassafras, shagbark hickory, hophornbeam, paw paw, and blueberry. These forests have a fairly rich spring wildflower display of rue-anenome, jack-in-the-pulpit, mouse ear chickweed, spring beauty, twin leaf, scrambled eggs, violet wood sorrel, Jacob's ladder, stonecrop, Solomon's seal, wild blue phlox, dwarf crested iris, and yellow star grass with one particular ravine that has a population of mountain laurel with the best wildflowers.

The riparian forests are dominated by hackberry, red maple, black walnut, honey locust, shagbark hickory, black locust, red cedar, sycamore with coral berry, flowering dogwood, redbud, giant cane, hazelnut, American hornbeam, rough leaf dogwood in the understory. In some areas of the bottomland there are some small wet areas dominated by sedges, rushes, grasses, sensitive fern, cattails, arrowhead, meadow pink, monkey flower, cardinal flower, boneset, joe pye weed, and water plantain. At least 198 plant species have been observed including one infrequent species, the butterfly pea.

Access: Open dawn to dusk for passive recreation including hiking, wildlife viewing, photography and hunting following statewide regulations, except that deer hunting is limited to archery and crossbow. Trapping is available by permit only. You must park at one of three small parking areas, two of which are on the right (south) side of Crooked Creek Road and the third parking area is at KY733. An information kiosk (board) is at the first parking area.

Red maples in full color at the edge on a lower slope at Knobs State Forest.

LaRue Environmental Education and Research Center

LaRue County Fiscal Court, 191 acres

The purpose of the LaRue Environmental Education and Research Center is to provide for educational opportunities in ecology, genetics, forestry, natural resource conservation and wildlife management. The Pearman farmhouse has been adapted into an interpretive center, and they have developed an approximately six foot wide by three-quarter mile long hard surface trail through the forest that contains more than 170 species of plants. The most significant forest stand is approximately 80 acres of mature white oak approaching old growth, as the previous owners only removed dead wood. While the dominant canopy species is white oak, 18 additional species have been observed in the canopy and co-dominant trees include sugar maple, tulip tree and black oak. The understory is dominated by spicebush, pawpaw, and Carolina buckthorn. While the forest is in good condition, there has been some recent disturbance from blowdowns and patches of red cedar and osage orange can be found as well. In addition to the forest, there is also a created native grass prairie and small pond.

Access: Anna Belle's trail is open dawn to dusk for hiking. From downtown Hodgenville, go north on KY 84/US 31E and turn onto KY 1794 and go approximately 2.5 miles to the entrance on the south side of the road. Parking is available at the end of the lane.

A young maple and fescue after the first frost at the edge of the mature oak forest at the LaRue Environmental Education and Research Center.

Letourneau Woods

A section of the Obion Creek Wildlife Management Area, Kentucky Department of Fish and Wildlife Resources, Hickman County, 951 acres

When atop the overlook at the Fulton County Library in Hickman, you immediately notice a large patch of forest in a sea of corn and soybeans to the northeast. Locally known as "thousand acre woods", this old growth bottomland forest has survived human disturbances and closely mirrors pre-settlement conditions. It is the largest contiguous tract of forest in the Bayou de Chein bottomlands, and is critical winter habitat for waterfowl, particularly mallards, black ducks, wood ducks, and green-winged teal. In one flight on a single day, more than 100,000 ducks were seen on site. But the site is also significant because it is old growth, with trees reaching more than four feet in diameter and growing 100' tall or more.

The majority of the management area is bottomland hardwood forest dominated by sugarberry, green ash, pecan, American elm, silver and red maple, sycamore, cottonwood, sweetgum and overcup, pine, swamp chestnut and cherrybark oaks. Drier sites have kingnut hickory, pecan, Kentucky coffeetree and black gum. The understory is sparse because of winter and spring flooding, but a number of vines persist including poison ivy, peppervine, groundnut, buckwheat vine, crossvine, trumpet creeper, Carolina snailseed, moonseed vine, burr cucumber, and roundleaf greenbrier. There is also a small amount of bottomland hardwood swamp, which is flooded most of the year and dominated by a few bald cypress, planetree, red maple, and overcup oak.

Dry slough, a cypress swamp, runs north south and the remaining forest on a narrow upland portion is coastal mesophytic dominated by sugar maple, black gum, black cherry, persimmon, Kentucky coffeetree, black walnut, white, chinquapin, red and Shumard oak, and shrubs including paw paw, flowering dogwood, witch hazel, red mulberry and spicebush. More than 137 plant species have been observed including four state listed species, the threatened blue jasmine leatherflower, and special concern blue mud plantain, water locust, and snow squarestem. The site also hosts numerous bird species including nesting cerulean, prothonotary and Swainson's warblers.

Access: Parking is allowed at gated entrances and no ATV, horseback riding, camping, or open fires are allowed. Open under statewide regulations for all hunting and trapping seasons. From Highway 94 in Hickman, take Bernal Avenue North, which will turn into Upper Bottoms Road. Go five and one half miles to a gravel access road on the east side of the road. Go one half mile to the parking area.

Mallard ducks taking flight from shallow water at the edge of Letourneau Woods section of Obion Creek Wildlife Management Area.

Lilley Cornett Woods

Eastern Kentucky University, Letcher County, Mineral rights to 166 of 554 total acres

This was the first old growth forest remnant protected in Kentucky, and is listed as a Registered Natural National Landmark by the U.S. Department of the Interior. The old growth forest occurs on 252 acres and while never logged, it has been disturbed by livestock grazing and periodic fire. The old growth protects an excellent example of a mixed mesophytic forest with 72 woody plant species occupying this forest community where American beech and red maple are the most abundant species in terms of overall percentages.

About 10% of the old growth area is mixed mesophytic comprised of sugar maple, basswood, tulip tree with northern red and chestnut oak, American beech, yellow buckeye, red maple, white ash, black gum, black walnut, pignut and red hickory, cucumber tree, and flowering dogwood. Beech forests, with some hemlock and yellow buckeye dominate the upper slopes and beech-buckeye forests with some sugar maple and hemlock occur on lower slopes and beech-white oak forests occur on more upper slopes with a northeast facing aspect. Hemlock forests with some American beech present are found on approximately 5% of the old growth forest on lower north facing slopes. Oak dominated communities occur on approximately 35% of the area, mostly on south facing slopes and ridge-tops.

In some stands on south and northwest facing slopes, white oak is the dominant species with some scarlet, black, chestnut, and southern red oak filling in the canopy. There is also some American beech and sourwood in the canopy as well. In mixed oak stands on east facing slopes, white oak is still the dominant species but there is some chestnut, scarlet and black oak present along with red and sugar maple, pignut and mockernut hickory, sourwood, and black gum. The ridgetop forests are dominated by chestnut oak with white, black, and scarlet oak, sourwood, red maple, downy serviceberry, and pignut hickory also present. A total of more than 530 plant species have been documented in various studies.

Access: Open to public only by guided tours from 9:00 am to 5:00 pm from May 15 to August 15, and during April, May, September, and October on weekends only. From November through April it is open only by appointment. No camping, collecting, hunting, pets or off road vehicles are allowed and picnicking is allowed in restricted areas only. From Kentucky Highway 15 south of Hazard, take Kentucky 7 for 13 miles and turn right onto KY 1103. Follow for 8 miles and the entrance will be on the left side of the road.

A large, mature White Walnut in the bottoms near the entrance of the main trail at Lilley Cornett Woods.

Lily Mountain Nature Preserve

350 acres, Estill County Conservation District. Written by Zeb Weese.

Lily Mountain is among the most scenic of many areas in the Knobs region, a range of hills which begin at the Ohio River in Jefferson County in the west, curve southeast towards Richmond, and then northeast towards Vanceburg and back to the Ohio River. This site provides views of both the forests of the Cumberland Plateau and the farms of the Bluegrass Region.

The site is largely forested and several ecological community types have been identified on the property including Acidic xeric forest, Calcareous xeric forest, Acidic sub-xeric forest, Calcareous sub-xeric forest, and Appalachian pine-oak forest. Woody plants at Lily Mountain include various maples, common serviceberry, pawpaw, hickories, common hackberry, eastern redbud, flowering dogwood, eastern wahoo, Carolina buckthorn, black huckleberry, black walnut, northern spicebush, and a variety of oaks.

There are several ridges and streams that dissect the preserve. Hikers will enjoy the rocky outcrops along the ridge trail, which overlook "Rocky's Roost." A non-profit group, the Friends of Lily Mountain, was established by local citizens to assist the Estill County Conservation District in on-site management, which includes developing hiking trails and providing environmental education opportunities. A preliminary, biological inventory has indicated the site is used by federally endangered gray bats and the state-listed Rafinesque big-eared bat. The smooth veiny peavine, a state listed plant of special concern has also been identified growing in the dry to mesic slopes. Diverse bird species may also be observed including black-and-white warblers, black-throated green warblers, hooded warblers, Kentucky warblers, ovenbirds, worm-eating warblers, and wood thrushes.

Access: Hiking trails and environmental education facilities are under development on the site. From Richmond, go South on US 25/Berea Road for 5 miles, then left onto US 421/Kingston Highway for 2 miles, then left onto KY 499/Crooksville Road for 10 miles, then right on Little Rock Road/Panola Road. The site is 2.5 miles on the left.

The view of "Rocky's Roost" from the ridge-top trail at Lily Mountain. Photo by Zeb Weese.

Lincoln Boyhood Home National Historic Site

LaRue County Fiscal Court, 228 acres transferred to National Park Service

This important site expands the National Park Service boyhood home of our 16th President, Abraham Lincoln. He lived at this location from age 2 until 7, and the land purchased with HLCF funding lies behind the actual home site and is a mixture of forest, a stream corridor, and a 7-acre agricultural field which has been sown to orchard grass, timothy, clover and alfalfa.

The lower slope calcareous forests are dominated by tulip tree, sugar maple, northern red oak, black oak, white ash, American beech, chinquapin oak, shagbark and bitternut hickory, and slippery elm. This is a rich north facing slope with a nice display of spring ephemeral wildflowers including bloodroot, trout lily, wild geranium, blue cohosh, jack-in-the-pulpit, wild ginger, spring beauty, dwarf larkspur, twinleaf, Virginia blue bells, blue phlox, Jacob's ladder, wood poppy, bent and sessile trillium, bellwort, and various violets.

The upper slope ridges and cliffs have a more open canopy with white, black chestnut, chinquapin, and post oaks with mockernut and pignut hickory interspersed with Virginia Pine. The understory has various grasses, shrubs, and flowers including broomsedge, Elliott's broomsedge, red cedar, black haw, smooth sumac, dogwood, hoary puccoon, bluets, dwarf crested iris, prickly pear cactus, shooting star, and green violet. The most significant habitat on these slopes includes a portion of limestone slope glade with following rare species Barrens silky aster, umbel-like sedge, scarlet Indian paintbrush, whorled horse balm, spinulose wood fern, blue mud-plantain, round headed bush clover, plains muhly grass, thread-like naiad, rough dropseed, and northern fox grape.

Access: Open dawn to dusk daily and special interpretative hours are available at the park's website. A hiking trail leads to the knob overlooking the site. From Bardstown, take US 31E for approximately 20 miles and the entrance is on your right.

Side view of Abraham Lincoln's boyhood home at the Knob Creek Farm.

Little South Fork

Kentucky Division of Water Wild Rivers Program, McCreary County, 23 acres

This land along the east side of the Little South Fork State Wild River corridor was going to be logged prior to acquisition by Kentucky Heritage Land Conservation Fund. It adjoins Corps of Engineers property, and the steep terrain has moist to dry calcareous forests with cliffs and outcroppings. The cliff and rock outcrop communities support two rare plants, the state endangered western false gromwell and state threatened Mock orange. Other species found in these communities include walking and cliffbrake ferns and Virginia winged rockcress.

On west-facing, drier sites, dry open forests with sugar maple white oak, mockernut hickory and slippery elm dominate with an understory of red cedar, Carolina buckthorn, downy viburnum and rusty blackhaw. In the adjacent floodplain, three rare species are found including the state threatened shining ladies-tresses, sand grape, and prairie redroot and in the water the state special concern Illinois pondweed which could have been negatively affected if the site was logged prior to purchase. The forests are quite diverse with blue and white ash, American basswood, cucumber tree, northern red oak, American beech, American elm, and white oak in the canopy with an understory of redbud, flowering dogwood, American bladdernut and American holly.

Several infrequent tree species, yellowwood and eastern leatherwood have also been observed here. The forests have a rich spring wildflower display of yellow fairybells, wild geranium, sharp lobed hepatica, dward crested iris, mayapple, bloodroot, Allegheny spurge, and yellow wake robin.

Access: Open to the public by foot traffic only, no ATV or horseback riding, and overnight camping and campfires are prohibited within 30 feet of a wild river. Hunting and fishing are allowed according to state law. Located off Jones Road.

Shining ladies tresses orchid is one rare species protected on this property adjacent to the Little South Fork River.

Green ash reflected in the Little South Fork River tract purchased with Kentucky Heritage Land Conservation Fund money.

Livingston County Natural Areas

Livingston County Fiscal Court, 2,430 acres in five tracts

These non-adjoining properties in the northwestern corner of Livingston County provide habitats ranging from mature oak forest, to cypress swamps, and steep forested bluffs. The sites include Bissel Bluff and Newman's Bluff Nature Preserves as well as the Wildlife Management Area tracts. Part of the wildlife management area adjoins Mantle Rock, an important site not only biologically, but also culturally and archeologically as part of the "Trail of Tears."

The original properties were purchased by the Nature Conservancy from Mead-Westvaco and then sold to Livingston County and are jointly managed by the Kentucky Department of Fish and Wildlife Resources and the Kentucky State Nature Preserves Commission, along with Livingston County. One of the locations has almost 400' limestone bluffs overlooking a forested valley.

There is a stream fed lake at the base of the valley adjacent to the parking area. The majority forest type on this tract is dry to mesic upland acidic forest on southern and west facing upper and mid slopes. The canopy is dominated by white, black, post and southern red oak and pignut hickory. The understory has hop hornbeam, flowering dogwood, Juneberry, and farkleberry. There are small, glade like openings interspersed throughout the forest, with a more open canopy with scattered black jack and post oak and farkleberry and typical flowers including goat's rue, Bradbury's bee balm, hairy skullcap, three lobed violet, flax, dwarf blazing star, orange grass and poverty grass.

On top of the bluffs are sandstone cliffs and detached boulders with white, black, and post oak, winged elm, red cedar and pignut hickory and a ground layer of poverty oak grass, prickly pear cactus, dittany, and various ferns including marginal shield fern, polypody fern, and pinnatifid spleenwort. There is a small amount of calcareous forest dominated by chinquapin, Shumards, and red oak, sugar maple, and white ash on more mesic sites whereas upland forests are dominated by chinquapin and post oak, redbud, hop hornbeam, and rusty blackhaw. Along the stream, the forests are dominated by sycamore, sugar maple, chinquapin oak, sweet gum, shagbark hickory, black cherry, and black walnut, with giant cane, spicebush, wood mint, and honeywort in the understory.

At another location, high limestone and sandstone bluffs overlook mostly second growth forest above Bissell Creek and it is more diverse biologically, although some of the habitats are similar. For example, there are dry to moist acidic forests dominated by the same species and the species found along the sandstone cliffs are similar. The herb layer in these forests have greater diversity of species including shooting star, upland boneset, smooth

Looking over one section of the Livingston County Natural Area from a sandstone outcropping.

wild licorice, shining bedstraw, woodland sunflower, dwarf dandelion, violet bush clover, wild yam, violet wood sorrel, Virginia creeper, dittany, elm-leaf goldenrod, small-lowered buttercup and summer grape. There is one small glade like opening dominated by farkleberry, Indiangrass, little bluestem, big bluestem, purple daisy, goat's rue and bird's foot violet.

In addition to the dry acidic forests, there are also mesic acidic forests dominated by northern red, white oak, sugar maple, American beech and tulip tree—level terrain black walnut, sweet gum, bitternut hickory, and sycamore. The other dominant forest type found at this location is the dry to mesic calcareous upland forest dominated by chinquapin, Shumards, and white oak, white ash, sugar maple, pignut and shagbark hickory with a diverse herb layer of Canada milk vetch, horse mint, goldenseal, southern buckthorn, pale indian plantain, pink thoroughwort, crested coralroot orchid, green violet, American columbo, small horse gentian, and several sedges.

Floodplain forest dominated by silver maple, box elder, sycamore, and sweet gum grading into pine, cherrybark, and swamp chestnut oak, kingnut and bitternut hickory, sweet gum, American elm, and green ash with an understory of giant cane, beggar's tick, false nettle, cupseed, sedges, spider lily, Indian pink, few-flowered tick trefoil and a rare vine (Cayaponia), which was discovered during the inventory process, dominates the plant community. The stream ultimately flows into a cypress swamp and associated forest dominated by cypress in permanent water and pecan, overcup and pin oak, bald cypress, swamp privet, American snowbell, buttonbush, bracted water willow, rice cut grass, buckwheat vine, large buttonweed, and climbing dogbane in more seasonally flooded forest.

The final tract is a mostly forested tract dominated by acidic dry to moist forest, with a substantial amount of mature to approaching old growth white oak. More than 500 species of plants have been documented on these properties including Price's potato bean, a federally threatened species, state endangered eastern blue star and five lobed cucumber, stalked wild petunia, state threatened Appalachian bugbane, and special concern Buckley's goldenrod. Livingston County Fiscal Court was awarded a KHLCF Stewardship Award in 2012 for their management of these sites.

Access: Open daily dawn to dusk for hunting, fishing in pond, wildlife viewing, photography, hiking via foot traffic only. No ATV, off-road vehicles or mountain bikes are allowed. Parking areas are located off KY Highway 1436 and Good Hope Cemetery Road off of KY Highway 1433.

Clematis pitcheri, an uncommon vine in Kentucky, was discovered at the Livingston County Wildlife Management Area during the botanical inventory.

Lost River Cave

Warren County Fiscal Court, 2.5 acres

The history of Lost River Cave is interesting and diverse, as it served as a place for Paleo-Indian groups to find shelter, water, and food; as a grist mill; as a camping area for both confederate and union troops during the civil war; as a bank robber hideout; and as a night club and dance hall. The purchase of the small amount of land by Kentucky Heritage Land Conservation Fund was to protect the area from future urban development on this busy, major highway in Bowling Green and to protect the important karst topography, this system drains 85 square miles, that is a component of the bio-reserve for Mammoth Cave and the Green River.

Ripley's Believe it or Not states that Lost River is the shortest and deepest underground river known and is supposedly 437 feet deep. The 68-acre valley protects four blue holes, which are underground sinkholes or caves with water and are often called vertical caves, and a valley (sinkhole) that was formed by the collapse of the cave entrance. The wooded ravine is very mesic and dominated by large trees that are at least 75 years of age including chinquapin, white, black, southern red, and swamp chestnut oak, tulip tree, black cherry, sycamore, hackberry, black walnut, eastern red cedar and osage orange.

This habitat provides ample habitat for more than 130 species of birds that have been documented in this urban nature sanctuary. The cave system supports a variety of cave organisms including bats during the winter, blind crayfish, and cave crickets. Humans have long used Lost River cave, and it was inhabited by Native Americans as early as 7500 B.C. for shelter, food, and water. In the late 1700's, a mill was constructed and used for grinding grain, wood carding and sawing of lumber, and it remained operational until it was destroyed by fire or flood shortly before the Civil War. In 1874, John Row built a new grist mill and distillery above the cave until fire destroyed it in 1915. During the Civil War, Lost River Cave was used as a campsite for both Confederate and Union forces and in 1869 the famed Jesse James gang hid out in the cave after robbing Russellville's Southern Deposit Bank.

In 1933, the first night club opened at the cave entrance and remained operational until the early 1960's. The cave then fell into disrepair for more than three decades, and in 1990 the Friends of Lost River Cave removed more than 80 tons of debris and began the task or restoring this important landmark that is listed on National Register of Historic Places. A master plan has been developed to restore and manage the site as a nature sanctuary by removing invasive species and restoring native barrens vegetation, developing interpretative trails that radiate from a new visitors center with various interpretative themes including a theater production, living in karst country, a discovery cave walk, the civil war oasis, tourists and the night and dance club, a mill hub and old Kentucky homestead hub.

Access: Open year round from 9:00 am to 4:00 pm except Thanksgiving, Christmas Eve and Day, and New Year's Eve and Day. A fee is charged for the boat and walking tours. Located in southern Bowling Green at the intersection of Nashville Road and Cave Mill road.

Looking out from the old dance hall into the forested valley at Lost River Cave.

Lower Howard's Creek Nature and Heritage Preserve

Clark County Fiscal Court, 346 acres

The purpose of Lower Howard's Creek preserve is to provide environmental education and to protect both the environmental and historical significance of this important forested gorge in Central Kentucky. Former historian laureate Thomas D. Clark stated that Lower Howard's Creek was the "most significant historic site in Kentucky" because it was where the "monied economy" started.

Settlers from nearby Fort Boonesboro moved into valley in the 1780's, and it was rapidly developed as water powered milling and stone quarry area with construction of Martin's Mill in 1787. By 1812, the valley was home to a number of mills and quarries shipping products to industrialized parts of the country, making it one of the largest industrial sites west of the Allegheny Mountains. The area began to decline after the Civil War as steam engines dominated the milling industry and quarries were located closer to railroads. Remnants of a mill dam, a mill race, quarries and small distilleries are found in the narrow gorge and experts in stone fences believe the area contains a greater variety of stone fence types and construction techniques than any other place in the Bluegrass Region.

The site also is ecologically significant and because of this significance, 228 acres were dedicated as a Kentucky State Nature Preserve. Two federally endangered species, running buffalo clover and gray bats, have been documented on the property in addition to state endangered grape honeysuckle, water stitchwort, state threatened white walnut and state special concern Missouri arrow-wood, Nodding rattlesnake root, and evening bat. This is a diverse preserve and more than 1375 plant species have been documented occurring in four distinct ecosystems. On south and west facing slopes sub-xeric forests have developed and are dominated by white ash, white oak, chinquapin oak, red elm, hackberry, blue ash, and honey locust, persimmon and lanceleaf buckthorn. Calcareous mesic forests occur on north and east slopes and are dominated by sugar maple, Ohio buckeye, kingnut hickory, white ash, northern red oak; tulip tree, sassafras, American basswood and a few beech with an understory of paw paw, witch hazel, spicebush, and exotic bush honeysuckles.

The riparian and terrace forests were heavily logged in the past and are highly disturbed communities dominated by early successional species like white ash, black walnut, red mulberry, black cherry, elderberry, American sycamore, box elder, sweet gum, green ash, and blue beech. The cliff communities are dominated by ferns including wall rue, cliff brake, bladder and walking fern with stonecrop, rue anemone, fire pink, late purple aster, and early saxifrage. On old homestead and farm ground, the plant community is dominated by red cedar with hackberry, honey locust, black walnut, black locust, black cherry, and Osage orange. The spring wildflower display can be spectacular with usual vernal flowers like bloodroot, trout lily, wild blue phlox, sessile trillium, hepatica, Virginia bluebells, and columbine. Twenty-two fish, 8 amphibians, 2 reptiles, 59 birds, 12 mammals, and 38 butterflies and moths have been observed. Clark County Fiscal Court received the KHLCF Stewardship Award in 2011 for their work at Lower Howard's Creek.

Access: Open only by guided hikes by staff or volunteers. The current hiking schedule is posted on their website. Located at 1945 Athens Boonesboro Rd., Winchester. To get there from I-75 take the Athens-Boonesboro road Lexington exit 9.8 miles south (KY 418) and the preserve gate will be on the left. From I-64, take KY 627 exit and go approximately 8 miles south to KY 418, turn right 1.8 miles and the gate will be on your right.

Virginia bluebells, golden ragwort, woodland phlox, and cut-leaf toothwort growing along an old stone fence at the Lower Howard's Creek preserve.

Marion County Wildlife Management Area and State Forest

Kentucky Department of Fish and Wildlife Resources, Kentucky Division of Forestry, and Marion County Fiscal Court, 1,993 acres

This relatively large unfragmented forest is mostly young, recently harvested and regenerating hardwood forest. There is less than 1% open land and because it is a large forested tract, it provides habitat for 39 bird species of greatest conservation need in the Outer Bluegrass Bird Conservation Ecoregion. It is typical knobs type habitat with steep terrain and deep hollows. The major tree species present are various oaks including white, northern red, scarlet, black and chinquapin, hickories, red and sugar maples, tulip tree, and American beech. Close to the management area is a rare siltstone-shale glade and one cave supports and endemic insect, the Tatum cave beetle. Because this lies so close to Lebanon and Gravel Switch, it was purchased to protect it from development.

Access: Open to the public and hunting is available under statewide regulations for all hunting and trapping seasons. Located off Siloam Road, Ed Sullivan Road, Penick Road and Tatum Lane in Marion County. The parking lot is located off Siloam Road. To get to the parking lot, take US Highway 68 and go 5.5 miles east of Lebanon and turn right onto Penick-Tatum Loop going south and take a right, going south on Tatum Lane for 2 miles, then turn right going south on Siloam Road for about a half mile. The parking lot will be on your right.

View of Putnam Knob at the Marion County Wildlife Management Area in the fall.

Marrowbone State Forest

Kentucky Division of Forestry, Cumberland and Metcalfe County, 1,958 acres

Kentucky's seventh state forest was the tree farm of the year in 2003 and has been under active timber management for more than 30 years. The terrain is steep, with narrow ridge tops and bottomlands and 96% of the forest is considered to be younger age classes with little mature hardwood forests which cover 97% of the land base. Both calcareous and acidic forests occur, and the overall forest is 17% White Oak, 16% Red Oak, 11% Yellow-poplar, 10% Hickory, 10% beech, 8% white pine, 8% chestnut oak, 6% sugar maple, and 14% miscellaneous hardwoods.

The dominant plant community would be considered oak-hickory forest that occurs on drier and upland slopes. These forests are dominated by white, chestnut, and northern red oak, hickories, white ash, sugar maple, American beech, tulip tree, black locust, black cherry, sassafras and red cedar. In more acidic sites, black gum, sourwood, chestnut oak, and Virginia pine become dominant. The other dominant plant community is a mixed mesophytic forest dominated by sugar and red maple, tulip tree, white, and northern red oak, hickories, white ash, Ohio buckeye, American basswood, American elm, black cherry, and black walnut. These moist sites have a rich spring wildflower display of white baneberry, leeks, chickweed, jack-in-the-pulpit, trout lily, spring beauty, wild geranium, twinleaf, ginseng, goldenseal, wild blue phlox, Solomon and false Solomon's seal, rue anemone, large-flowered white trillium, sessile trillium, and Sulcate's trillium. There are also some red cedar thickets and one old field that has reverted to a pure stand of tulip tree and there is one white pine plantation. More than 340 plant species have been identified on the forest. In addition to the native flora, the site protects habitat for diverse wildlife species, including the federally endangered Indiana bat.

Access: Open dawn to dusk for passive recreation including hiking, picnicking, bird watching, photography, and hunting following statewide regulations. Off-road vehicles, including ATV's, and horseback riding are prohibited. To find the forest from Glasgow, take the Cumberland Parkway to exit 14 and take Hwy. 90 (southeast) 20 miles to the Metcalfe/Cumberland county line. The main entrance is on the left (north) side of the road. There is additional access parking along Gordon Branch Road, Ed Turner Road, Lone Star Road, and Muse Road.

Red maple growing under tulip trees at Marrowbone State Forest.

Martins Fork of the Cumberland River State Natural Area

Harlan County, Kentucky Division of Water Wild Rivers Program, 1,594 acres in four tracts

This outstanding natural area connects Cumberland Gap National Historical Park and the Shillalah Creek Wildlife management area, and is 95% forested. The forest has been repeatedly harvested over time and at the present is young to middle aged. There are six natural communities present on the site, and a dozen state listed plant or animal species and a new state record insect. More than 788 plant species have been found including the state threatened Appalachian sandwort, painted trillium, crinkled hair grass, and Loesel's twayblade and state endangered brook saxifrage, Steele's joe-pye-weed, silverling, and state special concern species Curtis' goldenrod, and rock harlequin.

The incredibly scenic boulder strewn stream with one named waterfall, Quadrule Falls, is a moderately high gradient stream with low productivity, but there is one uncommon fish species, the stream shadow darter, and two rare dragonflies, the tiger spiketail, and Sable clubtail. Other rare species found include the state threatened Eastern small footed myotis and mountain midget crayfish, state special concern longclaw crayfish, and the state special concern Cumberland Arrow Darter.

Dominant forest communities include the linear mixed hemlock forest that follows the stream corridor and is dominated by eastern hemlock, sugar maple, sweet birch, tulip tree, umbrella magnolia and large thickets of great laurel. The Appalachian moist forests are quite diverse and north facing slopes have sugar and red maple, sweet birch, tulip tree, cucumber and Fraser's magnolia, American basswood, eastern hemlock, American beech, white and northern red oak, sourwood and witch hazel, with an incredibly diverse spring wildflower display of black cohosh, Clinton's lily, yellow mandarin, false rue anemone, large-flowered trillium, perfoliate bellwort and spikenard. South and west facing slopes and ridge tops are dominated by red maple, scarlet and chestnut oak, pignut hickory, black tupelo, and sourwood with an understory of blueberries and huckleberries, mountain laurel, with companion wildflowers of southern harebell, tickseed coreopsis, Indian tobacco, Indian cucumber and common greenbrier.

The driest sites are dominated by short-leaf, pitch and Virginia pine, chestnut and scarlet oak, red maple, downy serviceberry, sourwood, sassafras and blueberries. The dry sandstone cliffs are dominated by lichens, mosses, and three of the state listed plants. Thirty-six species of butterflies, including the Diana fritillary and Baltimore checkerspot, which are on the state watch list, have been found in addition to 10 amphibians, 4 reptiles, 57 birds, and 4 mammals. There is one significant archaeological site, Church House Rock, which has been heavily vandalized and was used for church services in the 1930's and 1940's. The Kentucky Department of Fish and Wildlife Resources and the Kentucky State Nature Preserves Commission assist with management.

Access: Open to the public by foot traffic only, no ATV or horseback riding, and overnight camping and campfires are prohibited within 30 feet of a wild river and on the nature preserve portion. Hunting and fishing are allowed according to state law.

Small waterfall on Martin's Fork of the Cumberland Wild River.

Morgan Conservation Park

Oldham County Fiscal Court, 255 acres

The goal of this park is to provide environmental education and passive recreational opportunities to the citizens of Oldham County. This old tobacco farm is a mixture of fields and woodlands that have been heavily impacted by past land use including grazing, cropping, mowing, logging and fire. The steep slopes support mostly regenerating, successional forests dominated by either sugar maple or red cedar and various oaks including chinquapin and red. Other forests are dominated by red cedar and black walnut and bitternut hickory. Other dominant trees found include white ash, hackberry and American basswood. Understory species include redbud, spicebush and coralberry. The remaining 24% of the land is in old agricultural fields or shrub thickets.

There is one small cedar glade on the property that has been heavily disturbed by erosion and woody species found in the opening include red cedar, redbud, rough leaf dogwood, southern blackhaw, fragrant sumac, and dwarf hackberry with an herb layer of false pennyroyal, green milkweed, croton, buttonweed, narrow leaf vervain, and various spurges. The entrance to the park on both sides of the drive have been seeded to big bluestem, Indiangrass, little bluestem, and various flowers including bee balm, black-eyed susan, New England aster, and gray headed coneflower. There are several ponds and streams that provide habitat for 19 reptile and amphibian species. More than 236 plants, 14 mammals and 59 birds have been observed on park lands.

Access: The park is open for foot traffic only on the developed trails from dawn to dusk. No ATV or off-road vehicles or horses allowed on the trails. From LaGrange take US Highway 42 east until you reach the intersection of Kentucky Highway 524 east, not 524 that takes you to Westport Road. Turn left, going north for approximately 1 mile and turn right going up to the hill to the parking area.

Gray goldenrod at the edge of a shallow glade like habitat with a young sycamore and red cedar in the background at the Morgan Conservation Park.

Morning View Conservation Area

Kenton County Conservation District, 208 acres

This old farm is a mixture of approximately 60% upland, calcareous forest dominated by various oaks, hickories, American beech, sugar maple, and ironwood with some red cedar thickets and woodlands at the periphery of the more mesic forests. The remainder is old fescue pastures and agricultural fields that are being grazed or cropped until a final management plan is implemented.

Access: No public access at this time until trails can be constructed and management activities have been initiated to control the invasive species. There is a small amount of frontage on the Licking River, and efforts are underway to provide paddling access.

Ironweed in a red cedar old field that overlooks the Licking River north to the Ohio River at the Morning View Conservation Area.

Mutter's Cave

Kentucky State Nature Preserves Commission, Barren County, 108 acres

The news hit in the spring of 2011 that white-nosed syndrome had just been found in a cave in south-central Kentucky. This disease was originally detected in a New York cave in 2007. Since its discovery, this devastating disease has spread to more than 17 states and has killed more than a million bats. Once it enters a cave system, bat mortality is over 90 percent.

The gray bat, a federally endangered species, is a very susceptible species because the entire population hibernates in only 17 locations across five states and Kentucky is one of those states. Much has been done to protect this critically endangered species in Kentucky, and more than 33,000 bats have been observed using Mutter's Cave as a maternity site. This preserve protects the cave opening, important entrance and exit pathways, foraging habitat along the creek and the karst topography lying immediately above the cave. The uplands are typical hayfields and little management, other than controlling access and some exotic plants is done in an effort to avoid disturbing the bats.

Access: No public access due to the sensitivity of the site for the critically endangered bat.

Passion flower vine in an old field located on the surface above Mutter's Cave.

Natural Bridge State Resort Park

Kentucky Department of Parks, Powell County, 471 of 2,250 total acres

This is one of Kentucky's premier state resort parks and was one of the four original parks dedicated in 1926. The entire park encompasses more than 2,250 acres, and the centerpiece is Natural Bridge, a 78-foot span reaching 65 feet in height. The Original Trail to the arch dates back to the 1890's, when it was a private tourist attraction owned by the Lexington and Eastern Railroad. The additions purchased by HLCF connects the park to the Daniel Boone National Forest and has four primary plant communities including dry, xeric ridgetop forests, mesic cove hardwood forests, streamhead wetlands and extensive cliffline habitat. More than 118 species of plants are found here.

A small amount of the forest is considered old growth, and most of the site was harvested in 1943 so that the remaining forests are approaching old growth criteria. State special concern species found include the sharp-shinned hawk and spinulose wood fern. In addition, three sedges and fairy wand, very uncommon plants are found in the wet areas. Ocoone bells, a spectacular wildflower and a species of special concern with the U.S. Fish and Wildlife Service, occur on the site but they are believed to have been planted by a previous landowner and persist today. The mesic forests near Townsend's branch and the narrows are typical cove hardwood species and include eastern hemlock, white pine, sweet birch, tulip tree, northern red oak, sugar maple, basswood, walnut, yellow buckeye, American beech, and white ash.

The dry upland forests are also typical of this region and are dominated by chestnut, scarlet, black and white oaks with pitch, short-leaf and Virginia pines dominating the overstory. Other canopy species include black gum, sassafras, red maple, sourwood, and pignut and mockernut hickories. The understory is dominated by various vacciniums, mountain laurel, downy serviceberry, and maple leaf viburnum. White's Branch Arch, show below, is found on this site. The wetland areas are dominated by royal and cinnamon ferns with various sedges, bulrush, mannagrass, silky willow, flat-topped aster, New Jersey tea, white turtlehead, and Canada lily.

Access: The Park is open daily for a variety of passive recreational activities including hiking and bird-watching. Prohibited activities include defacing rock formations or trees, hunting and trapping, disturbing, capturing or killing any animal, picking flowers or removing any plant material, collecting specimens, building fires or backcountry camping, rock climbing or rappelling, riding ATV's, mountain bikes or horses, hiking off the designated trails, alcoholic beverages, littering, and hiking with pets. The park's Sand Gap Trail traverses most of the HLCF acreage, and the Sheltowee Trace National Recreational Trail crosses the section across the top of White's Branch Arch.

White's Branch Arch is located on the property purchased by the Kentucky Heritage Land Conservation Fund.

Obion Creek State Nature Preserve

Includes Murphy's Pond (200 acres in three tracts of 1,601 total acres) and Wildlife Management Area (770 acres); Kentucky State Nature Preserves Commission and Kentucky Department of Fish and Wildlife Resources, Hickman County

This portion of the Obion Creek Wildlife Management Area is covered in a separate section because the State Nature Preserve and Wildlife Management Area adjoin each other in Hickman, rather than Fulton County (see Letourneau Woods chapter), and because the habitats are quite different.

The Obion Creek Watershed encompasses more than 206,108 acres in Graves, Hickman, Carlisle and Fulton Counties. Obion Creek is primarily spring fed and flows 48 miles where it merges with Bayou de Chien just north of Hickman, and then discharges into the Mississippi River. This area is one of five priority areas that are considered for protection by the U.S. Fish and Wildlife Service because of its importance to migrating waterfowl. It is also important because it is one of the largest remaining tracts of wetland systems within the state as cypress-tupelo swamps, bottomland hardwood forests, bottomland hardwood swamp, shrub swamp and open marsh are found in addition to deep soil mesophytic forests.

The area supports five state listed plants including the special concern rose turtlehead, and spinulose wood fern, and the state threatened rough pennyroyal, an ephiphytic sedge, and endangered blue-flowered coyote thistle. The southern twayblade, a historical species was also recorded from this area. In addition to the listed plants, three crustaceans, the endangered bleufer, and Texas liliput and special concern Cajun dwarf crayfish; seven fishes including the special concern chain pickerel, threatened taillight shiner, central mudminnow, and lake chubsucker, and endangered cypress minnow, dollar sunfish, and starhead topminnow; two amphibians the special concern bird-voiced tree frog and endangered three toed amphiuma; four reptiles included the special concern eastern ribbon snake and western mud snake, threatened southern painted turtle, and endangered green water snake; and three breeding birds, the great egret, fish crow and Mississippi kite can also be found in these habitats. 187 plants have been recorded in addition to 45 mammals, 40 reptiles, 30 amphibians and more than 200 birds.

The bottomland hardwood swamp communities are dominated by green ash, sycamore, eastern cottonwood and American elm. Close to the stream corridor box elder, silver maple, and river birch are more common. Typical shrubs include buttonbush and Virginia willow. Bottomland hardwood forests are dominated by red maple, sweetgum, overcup, cherrybark and willow oak with a midstory of possum haw and winged elm. The cypress-tupelo swamps are usually dominated by these two species with buttonbush, Virginia willow and swamp rose as a midstory but tupelo has not been documented at this location. The shrub swamp has a poor tree canopy and is dominated by buttonbush and Virginia willow. The deep mesophytic forests on the uplands are dominated by cherrybark oak, sweetgum, tulip tree, white and willow oak with a midstory of American elm, sweetgum, flowering dogwood and red maple.

Management: Work on stream restoration, creation of shallow water impoundments, monitor rare plants and animals, work on exotics, particularly a planted stand of loblolly pine. At one tract, bottomland hardwoods will be planted in old agricultural fields.

Access: The SNP is closed to public visitation except for Murphy's pond, which is often visited by students and instructors of Murray State. The WMA is open for public recreation including hunting and may be accessed via county gravel roads although accessibility is limited and challenging. Open to hunting, fishing, wildlife watching, and environmental education via foot traffic only. Parking is allowed at gated entrances and no ATV, horseback riding, camping, or open fires are allowed. To find the WMA, travel from Milburn one mile west on KY 80 and turn onto CR1124 and go south for 0.8 miles to the parking area. To access the WMA on the south end, go south on KY 307 from the junction of KY 80 and 307.

Cypress trees along the edge of Obion Creek Wildlife Management Area and State Nature Preserve.

Ohio County Park and Natural Area

Ohio County Fiscal Court, 100 acres

This addition to the Ohio County Park adjoins the airport and the golf course, and there are three primary habitat types found most of which is reclaimed strip mine. The natural communities found are a small amount of streamside forest along muddy creek that is dominated by sycamore, river birch, box elder, and green ash. This habitat grades into poorly drained seasonally wet forests dominated by red maple and green ash. The other forest type is the acidic mesic forest dominated by sugar maple, with some bitternut hickory, northern red and chinquapin oak, shagbark hickory grading into black walnut and tulip tree in the more disturbed sites.

Common understory species include spicebush, paw paw, hornbeam, hydrangea, and wahoo. The remaining forest has been dramatically disturbed and is regenerating with black locust, black walnut, black cherry, sassafras, persimmon, tulip tree and scattered cherry bark oak. At least 80% of the site is reclaimed strip mine dominated by the invasive exotic silky lespedeza with patches of autumn olive. At least 159 plant species has been documented from the natural area. Efforts are underway to improve habitat for the rare copperbelly watersnake.

Access: Open dawn to dusk daily for passive recreation including bicycles on both primitive and paved trails. Located off State Route 69 approximately one-half mile east of the Hartford exit of the Natcher Parkway.

Goldenrod and sumac growing in a reclaimed strip-mined area of the Ohio County Park and Natural Area.

Old Mulkey Meeting House

Kentucky Department of Parks, Monroe County, 19 acres

This addition to the state historic site was purchased to protect this park from surrounding development pressures from the city of Tompkinsville. The forested buffer is considered acidic mesophytic forest, with 50% of the canopy in sugar maple and American beech. Other dominant canopy species include tulip tree, white oak, shagbark, mockernut, and bitternut hickories, black cherry, red cedar, and white ash. The remainder of the forested species in the canopy includes red, American, and slippery elm, red maple, pignut, hackberry, southern red, chinquapin, and post oaks, black gum, sycamore, black walnut, Virginia pine and non-native loblolly pine. The understory species include paw paw, redbud, flowering dogwood, American hop hornbeam, American hornbeam and winged sumac.

The Old Mulkey Meeting House, originally called the Mill Creek Baptist Church, was created as the 19th state park and was established in 1931. It is the second oldest church meeting house in Kentucky, and was built in 1804 by a small group of pioneering Baptists led by John and Philip Mulkey of South Carolina. John Mulkey was a charismatic individual and preached more than 10,000 sermons and probably baptized the same number. He was an influential man, and four of his six sons went on to become preachers and his descendents were influential in establishing over 50 Disciples of Christ congregations.

The church was built in the shape of a cross with 12 corners and 3 doors to symbolize the Holy Trinity, and a historic cemetery is associated with the church and is the final resting place of early pioneers including Hannah Boone Pennington, Daniel Boone's sister. Religious services were held at the church until 1856.

Access: The Park is open daily from 8:00 am to 5:00 pm April 1 through October, and on Tuesdays through Saturday in November, December, and March and by appointment only during January and February. From Tompkinsville, take KY Highway 1446 approximately 2.5 miles south to the entrance on the right.

Inside the structure looking out into the forest surrounding the building at the Old Mulkey Meeting House.

Olive Hill Reservoir Preservation

City of Olive Hill, Carter County, 215 acres

This property was purchased because it lies immediately adjacent to the reservoir that supplies water to the city of Olive Hill and serves as a buffer to protect water quality. The 40- to 60-year-old upland forest, with some selected timber harvesting, is mostly dominated by various oaks including chestnut, scarlet, black, white, northern red, and shingle; and hickories primarily pignut and shagbark. Other co-dominant trees include tulip tree, black cherry, sassafras, black gum, sourwood, white ash, American beech, sugar and red maples and southern pines. No rare, threatened, or endangered species occur on the property, but it does serve as an important regional migratory corridor for birds because of the water source and adjoining forests. More than 69 species of plants have been documented, and typical upland woodland wildflowers like dwarf crested iris can be seen in the springtime. It is home to a variety of amphibians and water loving creatures because of the shallow water near the back of the reservoir.

Access: Due to fragile resources and water supply protection, this property is not open to the public.

Pinxter-flower azaleas bordering the Olive Hill Reservoir near the back of the property.

Overton Cave Conservation Easement

Kentucky State Nature Preserves Commission, Christian County, 55 acres

This conservation easement protects a vertical shaft for the cave that harbors a summer colony of federally endangered gray and state endangered southeastern myotis bats in addition to a winter colony of federally endangered Indiana bats and southeastern myotis. The cave entrance lies within a second growth forest of primarily acidic mesophytic and sub-xeric forest which comprises approximately 80% of the land area. The forests on the slopes, particularly east and north facing, are dominated by sugar maple, bitternut hickory and tulip tree with some American beech, chestnut oak and northern red oak. The mid-story is dominated by pawpaw and spicebush, and American hornbeam. The acidic sub-xeric plant communities are dominated by pignut hickory, white oak, chestnut oak, and slippery elm with some black oak and eastern red cedar also present. The understory is dominated by eastern redbud, Carolina buckthorn, hop hornbeam, and sassafras. Due to past land use history of logging and grazing, the herbaceous layer is not diverse or well developed. On the ridgetops the forests are more open and dominated by scarlet and chestnut oak and red cedar. The understory is dominated by Carolina buckthorn, eastern red cedar, and rusty blackhaw. Another ecological community occurs along the stream and are dominated by sycamore, black walnut, tulip tree, American beech, and sweetgum. The shrub layer is dominated by spicebush and giant cane. More than 133 plant species have been observed on the property and includes one rare plant, Appalachian bugbane, a state threatened species. Finally, one state listed fish, the Shawnee darter, a species of special concern, has been documented from Bull Creek.

Access: Due to site sensitivity and private ownership this preserve is not open to the public.

Indiana bats are one of the rare species found in Overton Cave.

Park Lake Mountain Nature Preserve

Fleming County Fiscal Court, 882 acres

Located in the Eden Shale part of Kentucky, this forested county nature preserve is located in an area with narrow ridges, steep slopes, and thin soils. The preserve is mostly young dry forest dominated by chestnut and white oak, American beech, and mockernut and pignut hickory with an understory or ironwood and flowering dogwood. The uplands are dominated by chestnut, scarlet, and white oaks, with mockernut hickory and sugar maple as co-dominants. The understory is dominated by greenbrier and blueberries. The herb layer is very sparse due to the thin soils and past land use history. In the bottomlands along the stream, the forest is more diverse and is dominated by sycamore, American elm, black walnut, green ash and red maple with an understory of spicebush, ironwood, and paw paw. The herb layer is mostly wood nettle, sedges and black snake root. The small, old fields are dominated by tall fescue and various exotic, invasive plants such as sericea lespedeza, white sweet clover, Japanese stilt grass, multiflora rose, and Japanese honeysuckle. More than 248 plant species, 24 reptile and amphibians, 35 birds, and 26 mammals have been observed at the preserve.

Access: Open dawn to dusk daily for passive recreation including hiking, bird watching, photography, etc. No hunting, mountain bikes, ATV's, off-road vehicles, or horses are allowed. From Flemingsburg, take KY Highway 559 east until it intersects with Kentucky Highway 1013. Turn right, heading south, and you will see the parking area on the right hand side of the road across from Park Lake Resort.

Young forest with elm, tulip tree, and sumac at Park Lake Nature Preserve.

Peabody WMA

Kentucky Department of Fish and Wildlife Resources, Muhlenberg and Ohio Counties, 34,560 of 60,000 total acres. Written by Zeb Weese.

The Kentucky Department of Fish and Wildlife Resources began working with Peabody Coal to manage Canada goose populations on its land holdings in the 1980s, and this relationship led to the purchase of nearly 35,000 acres. The site has nearly doubled in size since that initial acquisition, with assistance from KHLCF and a partnership with The Conservation Fund, a Washington, D.C. based non-profit.

While most of this property has been altered by surface mining to a degree, which makes restoration to its original habitat impossible, or at least impractical, the KDFWR has managed the site to create diverse habitats that benefit a myriad of species and to provide ample opportunities to experience nature via hunting, fishing, bird watching and other forms of outdoor passive recreation.

The landscape ranges from wet bottomlands to low dry hills with vast expanses of planted native warm-season grasslands. There are countless ponds and lakes created as a byproduct of mining operations. The undisturbed wooded areas are mainly maturing second growth oak-hickory forest. The site is particularly rich in bird life, and over 90 species have been recorded during midwinter bird counts including bald eagles. Short-eared owls have been observed nesting at this location. In addition, the site provides habitat for the rare copperbelly watersnake and many other reptiles and amphibians.

Access. Since this area is so large there are many access points off of KY 70, KY 369, KY 176 and US 62 in Muhlenberg County. A user permit must be purchased for access; they are available locally wherever fishing licenses are sold.

Roadside wetland. Photo by Zeb Weese.

Pennyrile State Forest

Kentucky Division of Forestry, Caldwell, Christian, and Hopkins Counties, 201 of 14,648 total acres in four tracts

Pennyrile State Forest is one of nine State Forests, and encompasses 14,648 total acres. The forest includes Pennyrile State Resort Park and borders Lake Beshear. This, like all the other state forests, are working forests and are managed following ecosystem management approach to demonstrate sustainable use while maintaining biological diversity and water quality. For example, one of the sites purchased with HLCF funding was clear cut, and the Division of Forestry is studying forest regeneration where an aggressive species, the Virginia Pine, is adjacent.

This site is regenerating into oaks, ash, tulip tree, sassafras, and black gum. Forest communities present include oak-hickory with beech-maple coves, acidic mesophytic, successional forested wetlands, cliffline and rockhouse. The acid mesophytic forest, which occurs below the bluffs, is dominated by beech, white oak, northern red oak, sourwood and sugar maple with an understory of serviceberry, redbud, flowering dogwood and sassafras. Spicebush is a common shrub and it has a fairly diverse wildflower display with wild ginger, white trout lily, squirrel corn, phacelia and toadshade or sessile trillium. The cliffline and rockhouse communities are typical, with hay-scented and marginal wood fern, downy alumroot, and wild hydrangea.

On the bluff tops the forests are dominated by scarlet oak, mockernut hickory, pignut hickory, and Virginia pine, with farkleberry, serviceberry and red cedar as understory trees. High bush blueberry is a common shrub. The final upland community found here is dominated by Spanish oak, white oak, scarlet oak, mockernut hickory, pignut hickory, American beech, red cedar, and flowering dogwood, with a sparse understory of Christmas fern, ebony spleenwort, broomsedge and the exotic, invasive silky lespedeza. The successional forested wetlands near the lake are dominated by sweetgum, red maple, sycamore, buttonbush, sensitive fern, river oats, and cardinal flower. More than 230 species of plants, 56 birds, five mammals, seven amphibians, and four reptiles have been counted on HLCF tracts.

Access: State forests are open to the public for hiking, wildlife viewing, hunting, fishing and other activities. Off-road vehicle use, including ATVs, is prohibited on all state forest land. To find the forest, take Exit 24 (Dawson Springs) off the Western Kentucky Parkway and follow Highway 109 South to Pennyrile State Resort Park. Pennyrile State Resort Park is located in the middle of the Pennyrile State Forest.

Copeland's Bluff at the Pennyrile State Forest.

Perkins Creek Nature Preserve

City of Paducah, McCracken County, 80 acres

This nature preserve is part of the Paducah city parks and provides visitors with access to undeveloped greenspace within the city limits. The nature preserve consists primarily of an old motorcycle tract that has reverted into grassland dominated by broomsedge, purple top, barnyard grass, Indiangrass, fall panicum and various goldenrods and frost aster. In areas adjacent to the forest near the creek, much of the habitat is growing up with young sycamore, sweet gum, red maple, callary pear, boxelder, river birch, and honey locust trees. The older, more mature wetland forest is dominated by cherrybark and pin oak, sycamore, and river birch, whereas areas where it is drier are dominated by younger forest with white and post oak, shagbark hickory, and tulip tree. Two state listed species, the state threatened red buckeye tree and the state special concern evening bat, were documented. A total of five amphibian, four reptile, 17 mammal, 45 bird, and 87 plants were identified during the biological inventory.

Access: Open dawn to dusk to foot traffic only from the Stuart Nelson Park or County Park or Coleman Roads. The site will eventually be incorporated into the Greenway Trail system.

Cope's gray tree frog blending in on bark of white oak at the Perkins Creek Nature Preserve.

Perryville Battlefield State Historic Site

Kentucky Department of Parks, Boyle County,
75 of 745 total acres

The purchase of a farm south of the park provides an important buffer to this significant historic site, which was the most important Civil War battle in Kentucky and occurred October 7-8, 1862. The battle was a tactical victory for the Confederacy, but ended up inconclusive as General Braxton Bragg retreated to the Stones River in Middle Tennessee to regroup instead of advancing on the retreating Union Army under General Buell. This was one of the bloodiest battles of the war, as more than 7,500 soldiers were killed or wounded and many of the soldiers were left unburied for days and were partially eaten by wild pigs.

The main park encompasses 745 acres, and the KHLCF purchased property contains "Old Mackville Road", which was a key transportation route as Confederate troops marched toward battle and some came back bloodied and wounded to be seen at a makeshift hospital. The purchase of the property protected it from a suburban development expansion of the community of Perryville. Restoration of native grasses to benefit songbirds and other wildlife species are planned for the tracts purchased by the KHLCF.

Access: Located on KY State Highway 1920 south of Perryville. The grounds are open to the public year round by foot traffic only, following a guided interpretative trail, and is not open to ATV or horseback riding. There is a picnic shelter, playground and museum and an annual battle re-enactment in October.

Cannon on top of fescue field on hill top at Perryville Battlefield State Historic Site.

Peterson Forest

City of Louisville Metro Parks and Kentucky Division of Forestry, Jefferson County, 103 acres

This former award winning certified tree farm provides an important buffer for Floyd's Fork Creek, which is one of the best streams for water quality remaining in Jefferson County. The project is an important addition to the Floyd's Fork Parks Project, which will ultimately protect and link more than 4,000 acres and 22 miles of stream.

The project begins at Shelbyville Road on the north and ends at Bardstown Road on the south. The Floyd's Fork Project will be interconnected via a continuous scenic park drive and a 20-mile portion of the Louisville Loop. Over 100 miles of new hiking, biking, and horseback riding trails will be created in addition to children's playgrounds, bark parks, accessible fishing holes, canoe launches, ball fields and other numerous facilities for family picnics and community events.

Pope Lick Park is also part of this project. The Peterson farm is located on the floodplain, with 10 acres of natural floodplain forest dominated by green ash, bur oak, and silver maple. Approximately one-half the farm was converted to black walnut plantations for genetic research and practical forest demonstrations. The remaining acreage is in open fields and buildings with road frontage. Once the entire project is completed, it is projected to protect more than 25 species of reptiles and amphibians, 40 fish, 20 mussel species, 19 mammals including the federally endangered gray and Indiana bats, 138 species of birds and over 450 species of native plants including the endangered Kentucky glade cress.

Access: Not open to the public at this time unless attending an approved forestry event or with permission from the Kentucky Department of Forestry or Louisville Metro Parks.

Walnut plantation in the bottomland adjoining Floyd's Fork at the Peterson Forest.

Pilot Knob State Nature Preserve

Powell County Fiscal Court and Kentucky State Nature Preserves Commission,
433 of 742 total acres

...on the seventh day of June following, we found ourselves on Red River, where John Finley had formerly been trading with the Indian, and, from the top of an eminence, saw with pleasure the beautiful level of Kentucke....

Daniel Boone
June 7, 1769

This eminence, or point, where Daniel Boone first saw the bluegrass, was believed to be on top of a 730' tall knob in Powell County that overlooks not only the Bluegrass region, but also the Knobs and Cumberland Plateau. In addition, the 280 million-year-old Pennsylvania sandstone, with lots of pebbles and stones incorporated into the conglomerate rock, was quarried as a source of millstones in the early 1800's. You can still see evidence of this historical activity and look out over Central Kentucky much like Daniel Boone did at this state nature preserve.

There are two trails located on the preserve; the one taking you to the summit is a strenuous 2.4 mile trek, while the much shorter Millstone Quarry trail is less strenuous and visitors can see millstones in various stages of production. The forest community is primarily dry, acidic second growth oak-hickory type with white, black, southern red, scarlet, and chestnut oaks dominating with pignut, mockernut, and sweet pignut hickory.

The understory is sparse with little ground cover. The lower oak-hickory forest is dominated by white oak and shagbark hickory but co-dominates include northern red oak, sweet pignut and mockernut hickory, tulip tree, southern basswood, red maple, sourwood and Virginia pine. The summit is typical pine-oak heath community with pitch and Virginia pine and white, chestnut, scarlet, blackjack and post oaks dominating with an understory of blueberries, huckleberries and mountain laurel. More than 202 plants including one state listed moss, 69 birds, 26 mammals, 14 reptiles, and 27 amphibians have been observed on the preserve.

Access: The preserve is open to foot traffic only from dawn to dusk, and visitors are required to stay on established trails. From the Mountain Parkway, take the first Campton exit and turn right, going north on Kentucky Highway 15 for 2.7 miles and turn right onto Brush Creek Road. Proceed 1.5 miles to the gravel parking lot.

View at sunset of the Bluegrass region as first seen by Daniel Boone from atop a point at Pilot Knob State Nature Preserve.

Milestones, large and small were quarried from Pilot Knob State Nature Preserve and other nearby knobs in the past and many are on display at the Clay City Museum.

Pine Mountain State Scenic Trail

Kentucky Department of Parks, Letcher, Harlan and Bell County, 500 of 2,000 total acres in multiple tracts

In 2002, the Kentucky General Assembly established the Pine Mountain State Scenic Trail. The purpose of the legislation was to purchase property along the crest of Pine Mountain for a 120-mile-long linear park originating in Breaks Interstate Park on the Virginia border to Cumberland Gap National Historical Park on the Tennessee border.

The trail would eventually join with Tennessee's Cumberland Trail to offer a 400-mile hiking trail. The trail in Kentucky crosses two federal areas and eight state public lands and will follow the Little Shepherd Trail in some sections. The trail crosses a variety of ecological communities described in the sections for Kentenia State Forest, Blanton Forest, Hi Lewis Pine Barrens, and Bad Branch State Nature Preserve. The majority will cross Appalachian pine oak forest dominated by chestnut, white, black and scarlet oaks with Virginia, pitch and short-leaf pine with sourwood, serviceberry, red maple, and sassafras as understory trees. The herbaceous layer has much mountain laurel, azaleas, blueberries and huckleberries. The trail is still under development, with plans to place an overnight shelter every 10 to 12 miles, develop access areas, information kiosks, footbridges, steps, culverts and other trail improvements. The trail is to be used for backpacking and day hiking.

Access: The trail is currently completed from Breaks Interstate Park to Kingdom Come State Park and can be accessed at Breaks Interstate Park, US Highway 23, or US Highway 119. Some of the trail follows the Little Shepherd Trail in Harlan County.

Mountain laurel in flower along the Pine Mountain State Scenic Trail.

Pope Lick Park

Tyler-Schooling Property, Metro Parks, Jefferson County, 282 acres

This historic farm had been in the family since 1875 when it is was deeded to the Tylers as a grant from the Commonwealth of Virginia. This land is part of the 21st Century Parks plan to protect green space and parkland along Floyd's Fork from development. It will also connect the Parklands of Floyds Fork to Cedar Ridge Camp. The park will provide passive recreation hiking, nature study, picnicking and canoe launching as the park protects 2,200 linear feet of Floyds Fork creek.

Of the 282 acres, 200 acres of the park are forested, and much of the forest is mature with several very large and old American Beech trees. The forest canopy is dominated by Shumards and chinquapin oak, white ash, and sugar maple, with some black cherry, hickory, American beech, and hackberry. Another section of forest that is not as mature is dominated by Shumard oak, black cherry, white ash, and eastern red cedar, with chinquapin oak, sugar maple, hickory and black locust as secondary species.

Along the creek the riparian forest is dominated by black walnut, box elder, silver maple and sycamore with green ash, hackberry and red maple present as well. There are some old fields in both the lowlands and uplands that are reverting back to forest. In the low lying areas, black walnut, green ash, red cedar, honey locust and osage orange are the primary species whereas in the upland areas red cedar dominates by some Shumard oak, black locust, persimmon and flowering dogwood are regenerating. Approximately 28% of the land in the low lying areas that was previously cropped has been converted to native warm season grasses. More than 230 species of plants have been documented.

Access: Foot traffic only on the Louisville Loop trail. From Louisville, take Taylorsville Road past the Gene Snyder Freeway, turn right onto South Pope Lick Road and follow to trailhead parking area or over a small bridge to the John Floyd Fields parking lot.

White snakeroot, ironweed, and yellow wingstem growing along an old stone fence bordering Floyd's Fork on the Tyler-Schooling Property at Pope Lick Park.

Putney Pond and Woodlands Natural Area

City of Prospect, Oldham County, 25 acres

Who would have thought that directly behind the city government offices in Prospect you would find a natural area? Putney Pond has long been known by bird watching enthusiasts, and over 118 species of birds have been documented from this small site in the middle of a city adjacent to a busy highway. Furthermore, who would have thought that this natural area would host the state champion Kentucky coffee tree, which has a circumference of 120 inches, is 105 feet tall and has a 48 foot spread?

Originally purchased in the 1930's for a hunting and fishing lodge, this natural area was threatened by development until the city purchased it for passive recreation including hiking, wildlife observation, and environmental education. In addition to the 11 acre pond and wetland complex, there are eight acres of mixed hardwood forest and six acres of reverting forest in this natural area. The forest type is mesic calcareous with a canopy of sugar maple, American beech, hackberry, white ash, black walnut, American basswood, American and slippery elm, and black cherry. Box elder and sycamore are typically found along the pond edge. More than 174 plant species have been found here but unfortunately 33 of these species are not native including garlic mustard, bush honeysuckle, privet, multiflora rose, princess tree, burning bush, Japanese barberry, winter creeper, oriental bittersweet, tree-of-heaven, and lesser celandine. At least 5 amphibians, 5 reptiles, and 14 mammal species have been observed and there is evidence of an over-abundant deer herd. There is one species of special concern, the Evening bat, which has been found at this location.

Access: Open via foot traffic only from dawn to dusk. No fires, alcohol, drugs and smoking are allowed on the trails and pets must be on a leash. Parking is available at several locations on US 42 between Timber Ridge Road and Fox Harbor Road. The trail system begins behind City Hall.

Fall color reflected in Putney Pond Natural Area.

Raven Run Nature Sanctuary

Lexington Fayette Urban County Government, 359 of 734 total acres

This nature sanctuary began when a 14-acre landfill on site caught fire and the state closed the landfill. The original nature preserve was created on 256 acres in 1977, and the additions from HLCF funds almost doubled the size of the park and it is now the largest city park in Lexington. The landfill was cleaned up and reforested in 2012. The nature sanctuary is dedicated to preserving the natural beauty of the Kentucky River Palisades, the flora and fauna found there, and early Kentucky history.

Raven Run is known for its outstanding spring wildflower display and has one of the best stands of blue-eyed Marys in the entire state. Mixed in with the blue-eyed Marys are bloodroot, twinleaf, nodding and sessile trillium, Dutchman's breeches, squirrel corn, yellow and white trout lilies, rue and false rue anemone, wood poppies, lavender waterleaf and wild hyacinth. More than 650 species of plants have been observed in addition to 207 birds, 25 amphibians, 21 reptiles, and 10 fish. The area is approximately 70% forested with two primary forest types, calcareous mesic and sub-mesic.

Dominant species found include sugar maple, white ash, Shumard and chinquapin oaks, bitternut and mockernut hickory, black walnut, black cherry, American basswood, Ohio buckeye, and American elm. The other communities include dense cedar thickets and tall fescue old fields, including some that are reverting back to forest. Several old fields have been planted to native grasses. Three distinct historic structures can also be found including Evans Mill, a corn grinding grist mill built on a rock ledge and vertical cliff in the mid-1930's until it ceased operation by 1850 due to roller or steam mills found in more accessible locations.

The Prather house is an early 19th century farmstead owned by First Sergeant Baruch Prather, a former Revolutionary War solider. The house was under construction in June 1800, and finished with a kitchen in 1812. The final structure is an old turn of the century lime kiln that was used for making quick lime for mortar, white wash, and other uses. There are more than five miles of historic dry stone fences in the preserve as well.

Access: The site is open for passive recreation only and visitors are required to stay on the more than 10 miles of trails. No pets, ATV's, horses, or bikes are allowed on the trails. Open to the public from 9 to 5 daily except Thanksgiving, Christmas Eve, Christmas, and the day after Christmas. Take Richmond Road east (out of Lexington) and turn right onto Highway 25 (across from Jacobson Park). Go approximately 3-1/2 miles to Jack's Creek Pike and turn right (at Judy Ray's Grocery Store). Go about 5-1/2 miles on Jack's Creek Pike and Raven Run is located on the left. A large chain-link fence and sign mark the entrance. Parking is available at the lot at the end of the park entrance road.

Purple phacelia along the banks of Raven Run Creek at the Raven Run Nature Sanctuary

River Cliffs State Nature Preserves

Kentucky State Nature Preserves Commission, Franklin County, 210 acres

This nature preserve was acquired to protect a large population (approximately 15% of identified habitat for this species) of the federally endangered Braun's rock cress and state listed Svenson's wild rye that occur on the dry, rock cliffs near the Kentucky River. The principal habitat for the rock cress is calcareous mesic forest, which is dominated by black maple and white ash, with northern red oak, basswood, American beech, Ohio buckeye, American elm, Shumard, white and chinquapin oak swith understory of spicebush, pawpaw, bladdernut, hop hornbeam, hydrangea, redbud, and flowering dogwood.

On lower, moister slopes, there is a rich spring flora with wild ginger, phlox, jack-in-the-pulpit, blue cohosh, white baneberry, nodding trillium, and great waterleaf being the dominant species. The other forested habitat present is a young successional forest on the ridgetops and upper ravines dominated by black locust, osage orange, box elder, hackberry, and red cedar with lots of invasive species like bush honeysuckle, autumn olive, garlic mustard, Japanese stilt grass, and tree-of-heaven. There is a narrow strip of riparian vegetation along Kentucky River dominated by sycamore, box elder, and silver maple with jewelweed, stinging nettle and hog peanut in the understory. More than 188 plant species have been observed on the preserve. There is a great blue heron rookery, with more than 50 active nesting pairs of herons.

Access: No public access except with written permission or on guided field trips by Kentucky State Nature Preserves Commission staff due to fragile resources and active resource management.

Great Blue Herons are common at River Cliffs because of a large nesting rookery located on the property.

Rush Island Watershed and Wildlife Conservation Area on the Green River

Kentucky Division of Water Wild Rivers Program, Hart County, 160 acres. Written by Zeb Weese.

This parcel has both ecological and historical significance and protects, Gorin Mill Springs, which is reputedly the largest spring in the Commonwealth. It also protects over a mile of frontage on the Green River. Several rare mussel species such as fanshell, clubshell, rough pigtoe, northern rifleshell, catspaw, pink mucket, ring pink, and sheepnose are occur in this more than mile long section of the Green River. Both federally endangered Indiana and gray bats are also found at this location. As with other HLCF properties along the Green River, it is expected to improve water quality in the greater Mammoth Cave National Park and its associated rare aquatic species.

In addition to the ecological significance of the site, this property protects the location of the Battle of Munfordville, an engagement historians have called a strategic high-water mark for the Confederacy in the Western theater of the Civil War. On September 17, 1862, Confederate General Simon Bolivar Buckner accepted the surrender of Union commander John T. Wilder and opened the road to Louisville for the South. However, instead of capturing Louisville, Buckner's commander General Braxton Bragg moved his troops to the northeast with plans to combine with General Kirby Smith.

Smith had just defeated the Union at the Battle of Richmond and Bragg believed their combined forces were needed to take Central Kentucky. This move resulted in the Battle of Perryville, a Confederate victory over Union Maj. Gen. Don Carlos Buell on which Bragg was unable to capitalize. Buckner was a native of Hart County and eventually became governor of Kentucky and pallbearer to President Ulysses S. Grant. The Civil War Trust has worked with the Hart County Historical Society to protect an additional 200 acres in the general vicinity.

Access: Due to limited access the site is not currently open to the public except by boat. Paddling access is available at Thelma Stovall Park in Munfordville; Rush Island is west of Munfordville.

Rush Island Watershed and Wildlife Conservation Area in the autumn. Photo by Zeb Weese.

Rockcress Hills State Nature Preserves

Kentucky Nature Preserves Commission, Franklin County, 65 acres

This is one of three properties purchased primarily to protect populations of the federally endangered Braun's rockcress and the globe bladderpod, a candidate for federal listing. Four distinct ecological communities, mostly low quality due to a history of grazing and logging, occur on the preserve and past human activities have resulted in heavy invasion of exotic plants in some areas. Ninety percent of the forested acreage occurs in two types: the calcareous mesophytic on steep east and north-facing slopes, and the calcareous subxeric forest, which is the majority of the forest type on this preserve.

This community is dominated by chinquapin oak and blue ash, with slippery elm and white ash as subordinate species. The understory is comprised of sugar maple, rusty blackhaw, Carolina buckthorn and rough leaf dogwood. Herbaceous species include dittany, wild comfrey and Virginia snakeroot. The mesic forests are dominated by sugar maple, white ash, and Ohio buckeye, with tulip tree, white and northern red oak as subdominant species. Spicebush and seedling sugar maple seedlings dominated the understory. These forests have a rich spring flora, with typical bluegrass species like Virginia bluebells, blue-eyed Mary, wood poppies, twinleaf, ginger, bloodroot, blue phlox, and various violets with white snakeroot, pale flowered leaf cup, and large leaf waterleaf flowering later in the year.

The smallest amount of forest is the calcareous xeric forest that has a semi-open canopy with exposed bedrock dominated by chinquapin oak, blue ash, and red cedar, with a midstory of rusty blackhaw, Carolina buckthorn, and redbud. It is in this community you find the rare globe bladderpod, and more common Carolina puccoon, and roundleaf greenbrier. At the bottom of the preserve there is riparian forest along the river dominated by sycamore, box elder, and silver maple with spicebush in understory and a ground cover of false nettle, cutleaf coneflower, wood

The federally listed globe bladderpod occurs at Rock Cress Hills.

nettle, and Canada clearweed. More than 186 plant species, four reptiles and amphibians, three mammals, and 30 birds have been observed on this small preserve.

Access: No public access except with written permission or on guided field trips by Kentucky State Nature Preserves staff due to fragile resources and active resource management.

Wood poppy and blue-eyed Mary carpeting the forest floor at Rockcress Hills State Nature Preserve.

Shelby Trails Park Annex

Shelby County Parks, Kentucky, 75 of 465 total acres. Written by Zeb Weese.

Riverfields, a local private land trust, holds a conservation easement on a 400-acre horse farm donated to the Shelby County Parks for an equestrian park and nature preserve. When an additional 75 acres adjacent to the park became available, the KHLCF helped the parks department to acquire the land to protect the woodlands surrounding an ephemeral stream corridor. Tree species in the corridor include shagbark hickory, hackberry, wild cherry, and several maple species. The upland habitats will be planted in native warm season grasses, including little bluestem and switchgrass, to create habitat for some of Kentucky's declining songbird's. A comprehensive biological inventory has not been completed, but no rare species are known to be on the site.

Access: Hiking trails are currently in development on the addition funded by Kentucky Heritage Land Conservation Fund. Over 20 miles of hiking and horse trails are available on the original areas of the park. From Simpsonville go north on 3rd Street, which becomes Todd's Point Road, for five miles and then take a left on KY 362/Aiken Road. The park entrance is two miles on your left.

Buckeye butterflies are common in late summer and early fall in Central Kentucky.

Sinking Creek

Kentucky Division of Water Wild Rivers Program, Laurel County, 300 acres

This stream, which is a major tributary of the state wild and scenic Rockcastle River, is considered an outstanding resource water by the state, is bordered on two sides by the Daniel Boone National Forest and includes more than three miles of stream frontage. The major forest type on the uplands, covering about a third of the acreage, above the stream is a hemlock-mixed forest with a canopy of 50% hemlock and 50% white oak, red maple, sweet birch, and tulip tree, and downslope with sycamore and American hornbeam. The understory is comprised of American holly, umbrella tree magnolia, and young hemlocks with Christmas fern, intermediate wood fern, and partridge berry in the herbaceous layer.

The other major habitat is fairly young Appalachian mesophytic forest with tulip tree, red maple, white and northern red oak, and mockernut hickory in the canopy. There is some Appalachian pine oak forest on the ridges however this is primarily a thicket as the southern pine beetle decimated the older trees. The highest quality natural habitat is a gravel/cobble bar in the middle of the stream dominated by hazel alder, stiff dogwood, smooth azalea, and Virginia sweetspire. More than 284 species of plants, eight amphibian, 18 butterfly, and 74 birds were documented during surveys. There are no state listed species found, but several uncommon species including Bailey's sedge, mountain camellia, and box huckleberry, have been documented. In addition, just downstream the shells of two federally endangered mussel species have been observed in addition to a patch of Kentucky lady slipper orchids. A portion of the Sheltowee Trace National Trail crosses the stream via a swinging bridge, one of only two swinging bridges on the trail.

Access: Open to the public via the Sheltowee Trace Trail.

Sheltowee Trace Trail swinging bridge, one of only two found in the Daniel Boone National Forest, over sinking creek.

Smith Watershed and Wildlife Conservation Area

Upper Red River, Kentucky Division of Water Wild Rivers Program, Wolfe County, 140 acres

This significant property is one of the few publicly owned tracts of land in the Upper Red River state wild and scenic river. It is entirely forested with a variety of forest communities, and over 189 plant species have been recorded. The primary plant communities found include a beaver pond with much cinnamon fern, various sedges, hedge hyssop, and bugleweed. There are large amounts of sandstone cliffline present, and both wet and dry cliffs occur and some common species include intermediate wood fern, climbing fern, stonecrop, hairy alumroot, and round-leaf catchfly.

On upland dry sites, the forest is mostly pine-oak forest and the southern pine beetle left numerous pitch and short leaf pines on the forest floor. Other typical species found here include downy serviceberry, mountain laurel, American holly, pignut hickory, and chestnut oak. There are blueberries and huckleberries in the shrub layer, and some common wildflowers include trailing arbutus, teaberry, forest tickseed, and Appalachian stitchwort. The most common forest tree on this property is the white pine, and it occurs in every habitat type except the driest site. The white pine mixed forest is dominated by white pine, eastern hemlock, and tulip tree and where present, large-leaf rhododendron dominates the mid-story level.

Other common trees found in this habitat include red and sugar maple, cucumber, big-leaf, and umbrella magnolia, sweet birch, chinquapin, black, and northern red oak, and black walnut. Other than large-leaf rhododendron, common shrubs include paw paw, witch hazel, spicebush, wild hydrangea, and sweet mountain pepperbush. Common wildflowers and ferns include white baneberry, jack-in-the-pulpit, hepatica, downy rattlesnake orchid, twinleaf, long-spurred and roundleaf violets, and cliff and purple meadow rue.

This community extends to the stream and there is very little typical riparian habitat, although some species like black birch, hazel alder, ironwood, and silky and alternate-leaf dogwood do occur. Wildflowers in this zone include spotted and pale jewelweed, cardinal flower, river oats, American water willow, wild sweet william, marsh blue violet and yellowroot. The final plant community, Appalachian subxeric forest, occurs in a band above the cliffs and below the ridgetops. It is mostly young, recovering forest of white, scarlet, black, and chestnut oak, tulip tree, red maple, and big-leaf magnolia. Mid-story trees include flowering dogwood, black gum, sourwood, sassafras, and hophornbeam. The shrub layer is mostly maple leaf viburnum, wintergreen, American holly, and blueberries and the herb layer is very sparse with few wildflowers except bluets. No rare, threatened or endangered species were found here except the Rafinesque's big-eared bat, which was observed along a cliffline. One uncommon wildflower species, the Canada lily, was found and there are few exotic plants present that pose significant problems.

Access: No public access at this time. Contact the Kentucky Division of Water Wild Rivers Program for updates as additional tracts are purchased.

Twin branch falls drops approximately 40' over sandstone cliffs to a small stream that empties into the upper Red River.

Springhouse Barrens

Kentucky State Nature Preserves Commission, Hardin County, private conservation easement, 55 acres

A conservation easement protecting this limestone barrens complex lies within a half-mile of Eastview Barrens State Nature Preserve. The privately owned property protects two rare invertebrates, the state endangered prairie gentian, state threatened Eggert's sunflower, Hairy fimbristylis and ringseed rush, and state special concern round-headed bush clover.

The glade openings are similar to those found at Eastview, and native prairie grasses little bluestem, tall dropseed, and big bluestem dominate the habitat between the rocky glades. The barrens and open woodland or forest surrounding the openings is mostly young forest but because of the complex geology, the forest is not well developed and would be classified as xeric or sub-xeric with a canopy of scarlet, blackjack, chestnut, post, chinquapin, southern red, and white oaks, pignut, shagbark, mockernut, and bitternut hickories, hackberry, red cedar with an understory of Carolina buckthorn, sassafras, and blueberries.

The open nature of the forest can be attributed to selective logging focusing on red cedar. Red cedar, Carolina buckthorn, and smooth sumac surround the glade openings and future cedar thinning and prescribed fires will assist in restoring more of the herbaceous species to these open woodlands. Some of the present thickets of red cedar, black cherry and hackberry could develop into mesophytic calcareous forests in the future. The significance of the site is the open grasslands that have the rare species plus a rich summer wildflower display of stiff aster, white false indigo, hairy sunflower, slender leaf false foxglove, wild quinine, narrow leaf evening-primrose, French grass, smooth phlox, slender mountain mint, small skullcap and pencil flower. More than 203 plant species have been documented from the preserve, and a very small percentage of these are exotics, although they present the largest management challenge.

Access: Due to site sensitivity, active resource management, and private ownership this preserve is not open to the public.

The prairie gentian, known from very few locations in Kentucky and an indicator of high quality native grasslands, grows at this location.

Spiked blazingstar and sunflower growing at Springhouse Barrens.

St. Anne's Woods and Wetlands Conservation Area

Campbell County Conservation District Conservation Easement, 165 acres. Written by Zeb Weese.

A century ago E. Lucy Braun, renowned ecologist, described St. Anne's Woods and Wetlands Conservation Area in 1916 as "the best depression forest on the Ohio River floodplain". In 1945, the Sisters of Divine Providence became stewards of the site as part of the St. Anne Convent campus. This religious community partnered with Thomas Moore College, Xavier University, Northern Kentucky University and others to develop an environmental education and research program on the site with a mission to "renew the face of the earth in maintaining and promoting a partnership with the land based on mutual respect, reciprocal healing, and reconciliation."

The Congregation of Divine Providence describe the site as "a gift of God's Providence," and state that "land and property are entrusted to our care as a resource for mission", and will continue their environmental education efforts on the site with assistance from the Campbell County Conservation District with protection of a KHLCF conservation easement. This is one of the best wetland areas along the Ohio River in Northern Kentucky and supports a diversity of native amphibian species uncommon in this region, such as Jefferson's salamanders, wood frogs and streamside salamanders, ravine salamanders, green frogs, Spring peepers, and American toads. The mature beech-dominated forest, with silver maple, cottonwood, sycamore, American elm, black willow, pin oak, and swamp white oak, provides a critical link in maintaining habitat in an area under increasing development pressure.

Access: From Covington take KY 8 (the Mary Ingles Highway) to Melbourne, KY. The trails through the beech forest can be accessed from the St. Anne's Convent grounds on the south side of the highway. A parking lot leading to the trails through the wetlands can be found off of Anderson Lane, which is on the north side of the highway approximately 0.25 miles from the convent entrance.

Trail through the beech forest at the St. Anne's Woods and Wetlands Conservation Area in winter. Photo by Zeb Weese.

Stone Mountain Wildlife Management and State Natural Area

Kentucky Department of Fish and Wildlife Resources, Kentucky State Nature Preserves Commission, Harlan County, 1,025 acres

This 94% forested natural area, which is adjacent to the more than 2,000 acre Cranks Creek Wildlife Management Area, protects a large un-fragmented forest habitat that provides important breeding habitat for forest interior neo-tropical migrant birds. Occurring primarily on the north slope of Stone Mountain, the primary plant community found is moist to dry Appalachian mixed forest where the west and south slopes and ridgetops are dominated by red maple, pignut hickory, tulip tree, scarlet oak, chestnut oak with an understory of mountain laurel.

The north and east facing slopes are dominated by red and sugar maple, yellow buckeye, sweet birch, American beech, white ash, tulip tree, Fraser's, big-leaf and umbrella magnolia, American basswood, white and northern red oak with a rich spring wildflower display with typical species like spotted and pale mandarin, large-flowered and southern red trillium, large-flowered bellwort, wild geranium, bloodroot, and speckled wood lily.

In one ravine on the northern end is a hemlock mixed forest stand dominated by eastern hemlock, red maple, tulip tree with some sugar maple, sweet birch and Fraser's and big leaf magnolia and thickets of great laurel. There is a sparse herb layer although downy rattlesnake plantain, partridge berry, two leaf miterwort, Christmas fern, foamflower and violets occur in this habitat. Appalachian pine-oak forest dominates the exposed narrow ridge tops with Virginia and pitch pine, scarlet and chestnut oak, serviceberry, sourwood, and sassafras, with blueberries in the understory.

On the southern most borders there are some dry sandstone cliffs that have a few scattered trees like serviceberry and Virginia pine with mountain spleenwort and rock polypody ferns. There are a number of rare species occurring within the natural area and include the state endangered Fraser's sedge, and southern bog clubmoss, state threatened Appalachian sedge, Curtis' goldenrod, and crinkled hairgrass, and state special concern rock harlequin, showy gentian, variable-leaf heartleaf, and jointed rush. More than 259 plants have been observed in addition to five amphibians, two reptiles, 58 birds, and five mammals.

Access: Open to foot traffic by the public for hiking, nature study, and wildlife-related recreation including hunting and fishing in accordance with Wildlife Management Area and nature

Aerial view of the Stone Wildlife Management and Natural Area showing the cliff face known as yellow rocks.

preserves regulations. From Harlan, travel approximately 13 miles southeast on Hwy 421. Look for a sharp curve approximately half way up the mountain on the right. Just past this curve is a parking area on the right.

Showy orchis are abundant in the rich mesic cove forests and are part of the rich diversity of spring wildflowers found on this preserve.

Strohmeier Hill

Feindel Conservation Easement, Kentucky State Nature Preserves Commission, Franklin County, 14 acres

The primary purpose of this conservation easement is to protect a population of the federally endangered Braun's rock cress, a plant named for renowned plan ecologist E. Lucy Braun who collected specimens from 1936 through 1939. It is known to grow in three Kentucky counties in the Kentucky River drainage and two counties in Tennessee along Stones River drainage and the Cumberland River. A total of 50 populations are known to exist.

The primary habitat this species requires is calcareous mesopytic forest, which is dominated by chinquapin oak, sugar maple, and white ash, with black walnut, Ohio buckeye, American elm, hackberry, and bitternut hickory as subdominates. The understory consists of spicebush and paw paw, and the ground layer at this site is dominated by garlic mustard and common chickweed.

Access: Due to site sensitivity and private ownership this preserve is not open to the public.

Lucy Braun's rock cress growing in its typical habitat on the Feindel Conservation Easement.

Tebbs Bend

Taylor County Fiscal Court, 185 acres

This habitat restoration project was initiated by the Nature Conservancy, and Taylor County purchased the property. It is part of the larger Upper Green River Watershed Project, which seeks to protect this watershed and provide for passive public recreation. The land was originally approximately 40% in upland forests on the ridgetops overlooking the Green River, and the remainder was in agricultural cropland.

Today this natural area, which contains approximately one mile of river frontage on a bend of Green and an island, still protects the ridgetop forests, but also has 40 acres seeded to native grasses including Indiangrass, big bluestem and little bluestem, 55 acres planted to bottomland hardwood forest with pin oak, bur and swamp chestnut oak, black walnut, white ash, and a 12-acre restored wetland.

There is also a cave on the property that has been mildly impacted with respect to water quality, and supports at least 23 taxa of aquatic insects. In the river, seven mussel species have been documented including the federally endangered clubshell. More than 65 bird species have also been documented from the natural area. The riparian forest along the river is dominated by silver maple, box elder, and shagbark hickory with sycamore and American elm as co-dominants. There is also some American beech, northern red oak, sassafras and flowering dogwood in the plant community.

As the forests transition to the ridgetop upland forest hop hornbeam, black cherry, pecan, sweet gum, and witch hazel are found in abundance. The upland ridgetops are classified as calcareous mesophytic forest dominated by sugar maple, American elm, Ohio buckeye, box elder, and hackberry with an understory of bladdernut, spicebush and some native canebreaks. As with most rich mesic forests, the spring floral display can be outstanding with alumroot, bloodroot, blue phlox, wood poppy, columbine, fire pink, jack-in-the-pulpit, dwarf larkspur, false Solomon's seal, sessile trillium, wild ginger, and Virginia bluebells proliferating.

The county has developed four hiking trails, mostly easy or moderate in nature, to allow the public to observe the differing habitats and wildlife found in the natural area. In addition to the ecological significance of the site, it also has historical significance and part of Civil War driving trail is on Tebb's Bend Road. There is also an 11.6-acre field, which served as a campsite for the 25th Michigan Infantry, and the banks of the river were used for loading and unloading supplies. There are also numerous signs showing troop movements that were associated with the Battle of Tebb's Bend, which was further down the ridge south of the bridge. The iron bridge, which crosses the river, was constructed after two covered bridges were burned, one by John Hunt Morgan's Kentucky Confederate cavalry troops and another in 1907. Today, a modern concrete bridge crosses the Green.

Access: Over four miles of hiking trails open to foot traffic only daily dawn to dusk. The parking area is located off Tebb's Bend Road and can be accessed from Kentucky Highway 55 approximately seven miles south of Campbellsville. The site is adjacent to the Homeplace on the Green River, an historic farm operated by a nonprofit foundation. An additional trailhead begins near the barns on the Homeplace.

Young green frog on longleaf pondweed in a small created wetland area at Tebb's Bend.

The historic bridge across the Green River at Tebbs Bend.

Terrapin Creek State Nature Preserve

Kentucky State Nature Preserves Commission, Graves County, 237 of 259 total acres

The first 22 acres of this preserve were purchased in 1992 with the assistance of the Nature Conservancy, and has grown in size primarily as a result of Kentucky Heritage Land Conservation Fund money. While the preserve only protects 4,500 linear feet of this small, 12-mile creek that originates in Kentucky and flows south into Tennessee, the surrounding habitat has various springs and wetlands associated with the mostly channelized stream. The stream was channelized prior to 1952 and over time has maintained many natural characteristics with gravel substrates and riffle pool development, which provides important habitat for fish found nowhere else in Kentucky.

A third of the 40 native fish in the drainage are considered rare and include the state endangered blacktail redhorse, bright-eye darter and firebelly darter. Other rare fish include the state endangered bluntface shiner, goldstripe and gulf darters, dollar sunfish, and brown madtom and the state threatened redspotted sunfish and central mudminnow. There are also numerous other unique and rare aquatic organisms found in this habitat and include the state endangered brook lamprey, the state threatened three lined salamander and Kirkland's snake, and the state special concern western lesser siren, bird-voiced tree frog, western mud snake, eastern ribbon snake, and a state endangered damselfly.

In addition to the unique wildlife found here, a variety of aquatic and wetland plants also occur in this habitat including state endangered floating pennywort, state threatened weak stellate sedge and American frog's bit and state special concern rose turtlehead. Because this stream lies in an agricultural area with intense farming, the biggest challenge is to protect the hydrology and water quality of this aquatic system.

Access: Not open to the public at this time due to the sensitivity of the site.

Wetlands associated with the springs at Terrapin Creek.

Thompson Creek Glade State Nature Preserve

LaRue County, Kentucky State Nature Preserve Commission, 105 of 169 total acres

Thompson Creek Glade is a high quality limestone glade complex with shallow rocky soils dominated by little bluestem and dropseeds, with big bluestem and Indiangrass occurring on deeper soils. There are four openings within the forest, ranging from two to four acres, that are considered glades. These are dominated by grasses and herbaceous species like tickseed, flowering spurge, dense and scaly blazingstar, hoary puccoon, gray goldenrod, whorled rosinweed with whorled milkweed, hairy wood mint, shooting star, small woodland sunflower, hairy lespedeza, prairie dock, and rigid goldenrod.

It is in these openings where the following rare species are found including, Barrens silky aster, scarlet Indian paintbrush, and Crawe's sedge. Scattered woody species such as redbud, persimmon, red cedar, farkleberry and post and chinquapin oak also occur in the openings. Most of the preserve, over 80%, is acidic sub-xeric forest with thin, dry limestone soils interbedded with acidic siltstone and shale.

The forest canopy is closed with white, black, chestnut, chinquapin, and post oak mockernut and pignut hickory with some Virginia Pine. Common understory species include flowering dogwood, sourwood, sassafras, hophornbeam, Carolina buckthorn, redbud, and winged elm. The remaining calcareous mesophytic forest is found on north and east facing slopes and typical canopy trees include sugar maple, American beech, tulip tree, northern red and black oak, white ash and shagbark hickory. Small trees and shrubs include paw paw, witch hazel, bladdernut, sassafras and wild hydrangea. More than 185 species of plants, six mammals, eight amphibians, two reptiles, and 32 birds have been observed on the area.

Access: No public access except guided field trips by Kentucky State Nature Preserves Commission staff due to fragile resources and active resource management.

Indian paintbrush flowering in spring in one of the grassland openings at Thompson Creek Glade State Nature Preserve.

Three Ponds State Nature Preserve

Kentucky State Nature Preserves Commission, Hickman County, 528 acres

Located on the Mississippi River floodplain at the base of the windblown loess bluffs lay three natural cypress ponds, two owned by KSNPC and the other by a private landowner. These bald cypress and buttonbush coastal plain sloughs, which have about 20 surface acres of water, are interspersed with bottomland hardwood forests dominated by boxelder, shellbark hickory, green ash, and pin oak, with an understory of giant cane, swamp privet, possum haw, and Virginia sweetspire.

Because these are natural ponds, they contain a variety of rare aquatic organisms including the state endangered cypress minnow, taillight shiner, dollar sunfish, and shrimp crayfish, the state special concern Bayou clubtail and state special concern chain pickerel and green tree frog. Rare plants found include the state threatened coastal plain sedge and state special concern water locust. Closer to the river, there is a small band of riparian forest dominated by cottonwood, silver maple, and black willow.

As you move up onto the loess bluffs, sugar maple dominates this mesophytic forest but other species including bitternut hickory, white ash, white oak, northern red oak, cucumber tree, tulip tree, black gum, black walnut, sweetgum, sassafras occur in the canopy with an understory of paw paw, American hornbeam, flowering dogwood, and spicebush. The herb layer has giant cane with a decent spring wildflower display of baneberry, green dragon, jack-in-the-pulpit, toadshade trillium and perfoliate bellwort. Rare plants that occur on the bluff plant community that overlooks the ponds include the state endangered clustered bluets and Tennessee leaf cup, state threatened small-flower baby blue-eyes, and the state special concern blue scorpion weed.

The other habitat that is found on the preserve is a former paper mill plantation that was been planted in sycamore, which is being restored to bottomland hardwoods. Rare animals that are found on the preserve include the federally endangered Indiana bat, the state threatened evening bat, and the state special concern fish crow and Mississippi kite. More than 178 plants, 108 birds, 14 mammals 37 fishes, two amphibians, and four reptiles have been documented at this site.

Access: Not open to the public at this time due to the sensitivity of the site.

Cypress trees and their "knees" which serve to stabilize the trees in the marsh and may assist with gas exchange during a drought at Three Ponds State Nature Preserve.

Tom Dorman State Nature Preserve

White Oak Creek tract, Kentucky State Nature Preserves Commission, Garrard County, 802 of 908 total acres

Named for Tom Dorman, the former director of the Kentucky River Authority who had the vision to create this nature preserve, The Tom Dorman State Nature Preserve totals 908 acres of wooded slopes and palisades along the Kentucky River in both Jessamine and Garrard Counties. This preserve has the largest amount of forested habitat remaining in this section of the KY River Palisades. The creek drops rapidly into a gorge, with numerous 10 to 15 foot sliding rapids for two miles from KY highway 1845 to where it dumps into the Kentucky River. The narrow and steep ravines above the creek are mostly mesophytic calcareous forests dominated by sugar maple and red maple, Ohio buckeye, northern red, Shumards and black oak, black walnut, shagbark hickory, black cherry, American elm, and white ash with an understory of paw paw, spicebush, Kentucky yellow wood, American hornbeam, and American bladdernut.

The east and north facing slopes have rich spring wildflower displays with wood poppies, dwarf larkspur, twinleaf, bloodroot, jack-in-the-pulpit, wild ginger, Dutchman's breeches, Canada white violet, and blue phlox proliferating and carpeting the ground in some areas. As the creek nears the river and along the river, the riparian forest is dominated by sycamore, silver maple, boxelder, American elm and cottonwood with spicebush, paw paw, and the state special concern arrowwood viburnum in understory. Spectacular views of the 300' cliffs or palisades, which expose 450 million year old rocks, the oldest in the state, can be seen on this nature preserve. Rare species found here include endangered starry cleft phlox and tufted hairgrass, threatened purple oatgrass, and special concern Eggleston's violet.

Access: The preserve is open daily from sunrise to sunset and is accessible via two miles of hiking trails rated moderately strenuous. The White Oak Creek section is closed to the public. From Nicholasville, follow Rt. 27 south for nine miles. After crossing the Kentucky River into Garrard County, continue for an additional 1.25 miles and turn right on Rt. 1845 and follow for one mile. Take the next right at Lambert's Chapel. Follow this road for 0.75 miles and do not bear left at junction. Parking is available in the paved parking lot at the end of the road.

The palisade cliffs reflected in Kentucky River as seen from the Tom Dorman State nature Preserve.

Tygarts State Forest

Kentucky Division of Forestry, Carter County, 255 of 946 total acres

This state forest adjoins Carter Caves State Resort Park and was originally purchased in 1957. The Kentucky Heritage Land Conservation Fund purchased additional land in an effort to create a larger contiguous forest with the state park. Overall, the forest is dominated by oaks including white oak (22%), Chestnut Oak (12%), and black oak (8%), and approximately 16% of these oaks are mature and are at least 80 years old. The remaining dominant trees include hickories (12%) and sugar maple (9%).

The remaining forests are primarily third growth calcareous and acidic forests ranging from mesophytic forests dominated by white, northern red, black, and chinquapin oaks, white and blue ash, sugar maple, buckeye, American beech, and shagbark and mockernut hickories in the coves and slopes to dry or xeric calcareous forests on upper slopes and ridge tops dominated by white, northern red, black and chinquapin oak, white and blue ash, sugar maple, buckeye, cedar, shagbark and mockernut hickory, tulip tree, and sugar maple. The acidic sub-xeric communities are dominated almost exclusively by white oak but other canopy species such as sugar maple, tulip tree, northern red oak, white ash, black walnut, red cedar, black oak black gum, and shagbark hickory also occur.

The old fields are in the process of regenerating to forest and are dominated by red cedar and Virginia Pine, with some hardwoods beginning to appear including tulip tree, black locust, white ash, white oak, sugar maple, American beech and black gum. The forests along the stream are typical of the region and are dominated by sycamore, red and sugar maple, buckeye, white ash, and slippery elm with an understory of ironwood, paw paw, and spicebush.

At least 463 plant species have been observed, and approximately 11% of the flora is non-native and the worst invaders include tree-of-heaven, autumn olive, and multiflora rose. Other invasive species found include Japanese stilt grass, sericea lespedeza, white poplar, and bush and Japanese honeysuckle. There is one cave on the property that protects federally endangered Indiana bats, along with big brown, little brown and tri-colored bats. During the inventory process, 26 birds, 17 amphibian, 12 reptile, and 16 mammal species were recorded.

Access: The forest is open for public recreation dawn to dusk for hiking, wildlife viewing, and hunting following statewide regulations. Off-road vehicles, including ATVs and camping is prohibited. From the south take I-64, then KY182 (Carter Caves Road) north through Carter Caves State Resort Park. From Wesleyville, take KY-02 to KY-182, to Oakland Ridge Road.

Large flowered white trillium in bloom at Tygart State Forest.

Upper Green River Biological Reserve

Western Kentucky University and Kentucky Division of Water Wild Rivers Program, Hart County, 1,142 acres

The upper Green River is one of the most biologically important rivers remaining in eastern North America, and the WKU Bioreserve and wild rivers properties adjoin one another and protect more than 1.6 miles of river frontage on both banks of the river. The preserve lies approximately two miles upstream from Mammoth Cave National Park, which is one of the most biologically diverse parks in North America.

The upper Green is noted for its high diversity of freshwater organisms, including 109 fish and 60 mussel species. Lands protected in the preserve surround several mussel beds that harbor a number of federally endangered mussels including the fanshell, northern rifleshell, ring pink, clubshell, rough pigtoe and state endangered spectaclecase, pocketbook, and pyramid pigtoe. In one spring on the northern edge of the preserve, McCoy's blue hole, the federally endangered Mammoth cave shrimp has been documented.

Because of the significance of this site for the aquatic life it supports, one of the primary objectives for protecting this habitat is to protect water quality. To achieve this goal, they have closed and capped oil wells and removed storage tanks and flow lines, eliminated gravel mining in the mussel beds and shoals, eliminated cattle grazing and restored bottomland hardwood forest along the river to prevent erosion, and control non-point source pollution by restoring upland forest and barrens.

In addition to the aquatic habitats in the river, the preserve also supports a variety of upland habitats ranging from bottomland hardwoods to limestone barrens and glades to mesic and oak-hickory forests and restored prairie and barrens. More than 600 plant species have been found here including some uncommon species like heartleaf noseburn and southern shagbark hickory. A number of rare plants, including Eggert's sunflower, royal catchfly, starry cleft phlox, and showy lady slipper orchid have been restored to the property.

Upland habitats vary, from young evergreen forests dominated by Virginia or loblolly pine, and red cedar on the tops of knobs that can grade into limestone glades that are dominated by red cedar with aromatic sumac and southern blackhaw with diverse herb layer of agave, nodding onion, glade coneflower, hoary puccoon, prickly pear cactus, sandwort, prairie tea, flowering spurge, glade st. johns wort, bird's foot violet, button blazingstar, eastern whiteflower beard tongue, gray coneflower, wild petunia and short grasses little bluestem and various dropseeds. There is one small barrens with typical grassland species including little bluestem, big bluestem and Indiangrass with

Overview of the Upper Green River Biological Reserve showing an important freshwater mussel bed in the Green in the foreground, forested lands bordering the river, and re-planted riparian forest and upland prairie on the right.

hairy sunflower, rattlesnake master, agave, button blazingstar, glade coneflower, bergamot, greater tickseed, gray coneflower, and whorled rosinweed.

The upland dry forests are dominated by chinquapin, white, black, and Shumard oaks, sugar maple, shagbark hickory, and white and blue ash on calcareous soils and on sandstone soils the dominant species are chestnut, black, and red oak. Mesic forests are dominated by sugar maple, Ohio buckeye, American beech, white and blue ash, tulip tree, red and chinquapin oak, and American basswood with an understory of paw paw, wild hydrangea, hop hornbeam, and bladdernut.

The bottomland hardwood forests are dominated by sycamore, box elder, silver maple, green ash, black walnut, American elm, hornbeam with an understory of giant cane and spicebush with various asters, sedges, wild ryes, and hog peanut in the herb layer.

In the river on the gravel or cobble areas, various asters, river oats, water willow, smart weeds, rice grass, buttonweed, wild rye grasses, fringed loosestrife, goldenrods, and indigo bush can be found. These terrestrial habitats support more than 95 bird species, numerous mammals including the gray bat, a federally endangered species and the Allegheny wood rat, an uncommon species, and 151 butterflies and moths including the Olympia marble butterfly, which only occurs in two other locations in Kentucky. WKU received the inaugural KHLCF Stewardship award in 2008 for their management efforts on the Green River in cooperation with the Kentucky Division of Water Wild Rivers Program.

Access: Because of the sensitivity of the site and because Western Kentucky University uses the facility to provide an outdoor lab for research and environmental education, this is open only by contacting the preserve manager at Western Kentucky University.

The green river as it flows past land purchased by Kentucky Division of Water, Wild Rivers Program and Western Kentucky University.

Whitley Branch Wetland

City of London, Laurel County, 85 acres

This property was purchased to restore a wetland and its hydrology to a meandering stream channel that has been highly impacted by development and contamination. This particular branch has been identified as the primary source of nutrients, sediments, pollution, and pathogens in the Corbin City Reservoir watershed. The current vegetation supports primarily tall fescue and old field goldenrod, with some patches of swamp rose and blackberries. Woody vegetation present includes red maple, sweet gum, and silver maple with some sycamore. The vegetation will be restored to more native species including pin oak, white, swamp chestnut, and willow oaks along with naturally regenerating green ash, black willow, red maple, and silver maple.

Access: Not open to the public at the present time due to wetland restoration activities. It will be open in the future for environmental education activities.

Swamp rose and sweet gum covered in lichens at the Whitley Branch Wetland.

William H. Martin Watershed and Wildlife Conservation Area

Rockcastle River, Kentucky Division of Water Wild Rivers Program, Pulaski County, 459 acres. Written by Zeb Weese.

This property protects most of the watershed of Beech Bingham Branch as it flows into the Rockcastle River. It is named for Dr. William H. Martin, the founding chairman of the Kentucky Heritage Land Conservation Fund Board and Professor at Eastern Kentucky University. This namesake preserve protects nearly 500 acres of various forest communities, which was the focus of Dr. Martin's studies. The site is characterized by a ravine and riparian forest dominated by eastern hemlock. An extensive sandstone cliffline is present here above the mixed hardwood and riparian forests.

While a complete biological inventory has not been completed, potential plant species of interest include populations of Kentucky lady slipper, Southern bog goldenrod, sand grape, and sweet fern, which are known from adjacent sites. Immediately downstream of the site, the federally endangered Cumberland bean pearly-mussel and the imperiled ashy darter have been documented. This forest also provides potential summer roosting habitat for the federally endangered Indiana bat and several other bat species.

Access: This site is adjacent to the Daniel Boone National Forest and near the Bee Rock Campground located at the Highway 192 Bridge as it crosses the Rockcastle River on the Pulaski and Laurel County line.No public access at this time. Contact the Kentucky Division of Water Wild Rivers Program for updates as additional tracts are purchased.

Beech Bingham Branch flows into the Rockcastle River on the William H. Martin Watershed and Wildlife Conservation Area. Photo by Joe Dietz.

Kentucky Lady Slippers are known to occur in several locations in the alluvial bottoms of the Rockcastle River and its tributaries.

William Whitley House and Sportsman Hill

Kentucky Department of Parks, Lincoln County, 80 acres in two tracts

The purchase of several tall fescue old fields surrounding the original 40-acre park site has tripled the size of this state historic site, which contains the first brick home built in Kentucky. If you look out a front window, you can see the location of the first horse race course in Kentucky, Sportsman Hill. The circular track was built of clay, not grass, and ran counter clockwise, the opposite of what would be expected in the mother country. The house was completed in 1794 and was used as both a home and fortress against Native Americans, evidenced by the secret staircase and windowless kitchen with a false ceiling that provided a secret hiding location. Many notables were visitors to the home including Daniel Boone and George Rogers Clark. Restoration of native grasses to benefit songbirds and other wildlife species are planned for the tracts purchased by the KHLCF.

Access: The home is open from April through October on fee based guided tours. Winter tours are based on weather. The grounds are open to the public by foot traffic only, not ATV or horseback riding and there are two picnic shelters and a playground. From US Highway 150 turn south onto Kentucky 1369 and turn left onto William Whitley Road for 0.6 miles. The park is on the right.

William Whitley House State Historic Site.

Wyatt Jefferies Woods

Green County Fiscal Court, 58 acres

This small forest is believed to be the last old growth forest located in this part of the state. It is a unique type of forest called a flatwoods, which occurs in broad flats with fragipan soils that impede the downward migration of water, which results in standing water during periods of the year. It is believed that fire was an important component of this area, which resulted in a more open-canopied forest.

Two forest types are known in the woods. The first include well-drained flatwoods, dominated by American beech and white oak with Southern red and black oaks, tulip tree, sweet gum, black gum, red maple, pignut and shellbark hickory with a sparse understory of pawpaw, flowering dogwood, Carolina buckthorn, and strawberry bush. The other type found here is the poorly drained flatwoods, and more water loving species dominate the canopy and include red maple, sweetgum, and blackgum. There are several small sinkholes and one depression that hold water during most of the year. More than 118 plant species have been observed and 17 species of amphibians.

Access: Open to public dawn to dusk and the trailhead can be accessed from the parking area on US 68. It is open to foot traffic only and visitors must stay on trails. From Greensburg, go 7.5 miles south on US 68 and the parking lot will be on your left just past H. Patterson Road.

Flowering dogwood in fall color at the edge of Wyatt Jefferies Woods.

Yellow Creek Park

Daviess County Fiscal Court, Kentucky, 1.4 of 152 total acres

The small purchase of land immediately adjacent to the natural area provides additional buffer to encroaching development, which is a major threat. The natural area of this park is mostly forested along the banks of Yellow Creek and more than 62 species of wildflowers and 19 tree species have been observed. In addition, 20 mammals and 90 birds have been recorded. This park is noted for its exceptional spring wildflower display, particularly on wildflower hill that boasts 20 species and harbors one of the largest populations of recurved trillium in the state.

The riparian floodplain forest and moist slope forest is dominated by sassafras, sweet gum, black gum, hackberry, black walnut, box elder, sugar maple, northern red and white oak, American elm, tulip tree, sycamore, and white ash. In addition to providing a buffer against future development, the addition also provides access to a restored African-American one-room Rosenwald School. Other features of the natural area include hiking trails with two reconstructed covered walking bridges over the creek, a swinging bridge, and a nature center where environmental education programs are conducted.

Access: Hiking trails are open to the public from 8:00 am to 11:00 pm in the summer, and from 8:00 am to 5:00 pm in the winter. From Owensboro take US Highway 231 east until it intersects with KY Highway 144. Turn right and go approximately one mile, and the park entrance will be on the right.

Recurved trillium and mayapple growing together at Yellow Creek Park.

Yellowbank Wildlife Management Area

Kentucky Department of Fish and Wildlife Resources, Breckinridge County, Kentucky
1,332 of 6,775 total acres in two tracts

This management area is 85% forested, 11% open fields and pastures, 3% wetland and 1% open water. It is located adjacent to the Ohio River, and one tract purchased with HLCF funding is mostly early successional second growth forest and riparian forest bordering Town Creek. The other has a variety of habitats ranging from dry upland forests with cliffs to riparian forests and riparian or wetland communities along the Ohio River.

In the mesic acidic forests, the spring wildflowers can be profuse and abundant with large patches of blue-eyed Mary, wood poppy, recurved trillium, Virginia spiderwort, jack-in-the-pulpit, bloodroot, stonecrop, wild comfrey, false dandelion, and veined skullcap. More than 159 plant species including state special concern species French's shooting star have been observed. In addition, 40 breeding birds, 13 mammals including federally endangered gray and Indiana bats and the state listed Rafinesque big-eared bats, and 58 species of reptiles and amphibians including the state special concern green tree frog.

There are a variety of forested habitats on the management area ranging from upland acidic sub-xeric forest dominated by white oak, tulip tree, sugar maple, black gum, scarlet, black oak and northern red oak, sassafras, shagbark and mockernut hickories to acidic mesophytic forests of the ravines and lower slopes dominated by sugar maple, white ash, black walnut, American elm, beech, tulip tree, white oak, shagbark and pignut hickories. Riparian forests along river are dominated by box elder, black walnut and hackberry with some black locus and black cherry.

One small section of the area has rock shelters and dry sandstone cliffs. Mudflat/sandbar communities along the shoreline are dominated by false indigo, silver maple, sandbar and black willow with buttonweed, water willow, anglepod milkvine, burcucumber, old-field aster, mugwort, riverbank goldenrod, Jerusalem artichoke and eastern lined and goblet asters. The backwater sloughs are dominated by buttonbush and silver maple, with basket oak, sugarberry, boxelder, green ash, sweetgum, and sycamore.

Access: Open to the public daily according to statewide wildlife management area regulations with some noted changes including special restrictions for deer hunting. Hiking trails across from information station on Hwy 259 and a 1.2-mile loop trail accessed from center of WMA are open dawn to dusk. A 20-stop archery trail (3/4-mile loop) located at the end of campground is open to public. Fishing is allowed in area ponds and on Yellowbank Creek, and the ramp at creek, which allows access to Ohio River. Tract 1 is closed from October 15 through March 15 as a waterfowl refuge. Primitive camping is allowed on designated sites only.

Rare French's shooting star growing under the cliff at Yellowbank Wildlife Management Area.

The Future

What does the future hold for nature conservation in Kentucky? That is a really good question without a really good answer, for there are so many variables that can affect the outcome.

I, like many others, am cautiously optimistic or perhaps being a pessimistic optimist because if nothing else, Nature is certainly resilient. If we look at the history of the last few decades you could get depressed very quickly, as Kentucky continues to fall behind in many categories with respect to the environment. Forbes ranked Kentucky as the 4th worst state for the environment in the country, and Wall Street 24/7 rated us as the 10th worst "Green State."

We continue to support our extractive industries at the expense of natural areas, which has resulted in our rankings as 4th worst for toxic air pollution, 6th worst for mercury pollution, 6th in release of harmful human development toxins, 7th worst in release of cancer causing chemicals, 9th worst in release of reproductive toxins, and 11th worst for carbon dioxide emissions as a result of burning fossil fuels. To top all that off, we can claim the top spot for trashing our public lands. The result is that more species in the state are being added to the Federal Threatened and Endangered list, and declining budgets for governmental agencies like the Kentucky Division of Forestry, Nature Preserves Commission, Division of Water, etc., from the economic downturn over the past decade will affect conservation efforts.

On the positive side, the elk herd continues to grow, forests continue to grow more stock and we are moving closer to sustainable forestry, lands are being purchased by private groups such as the Kentucky Natural Lands Trust, and there are signs of hope on the horizon. The state altered the Heritage Land Conservation Program such that private entities can apply to purchase land with matching dollars; perhaps a small portion of the sales tax on outdoor and recreational equipment can be used to purchase conservation lands, and maybe even some of the revenue from expanding gaming could be used for conservation.

Whatever the future holds, we do know that the HLCF will continue to be the primary source of funding for land conservation in the near future. Hopefully we can hang in there until the economy turns around and conservation funding returns to some level that agencies can at least do their jobs and find those unique properties that deserve special protection. In the end, it depends on ***all*** of us to support conservation activities to ensure a healthy environment for generations of future Kentuckians.

References

1. National Wilderness Institute, 1995, (http://www.nwi.org/Maps/LandChart.html).

2. Zourarakis, D.P., 2009. Land cover change entropy: the 2001-2005 International Workshop on the Analysis of Mulit-temporal Remote Sensing Images, July 28-30, Groton, Connecticut, USA.

3. Eric M. White, A.T. Morzillob, and R. J. Aliga, 2008. Past and projected rural land conversion in the US at state, regional, and national levels. Landscape and Urban Planning 89 (2009) 37-48.

4. U.S. EPA., 2012. Wetlands-Status and Trends, http://water.epa.gov/type/wetlands/vital_status.cfm

5. Abernathy, G.D. White, E. Laudermilk, and M. Evans, 2010. Kentucky's Natural Heritage: An Illustrated Guide to Biodiversity. University Press of Kentucky, 200 pp.

6. Pimentel, D., R. Zuniga, and D. Morrison, 2005. Update on the environmental and economic costs associated with alien-invasive species in the United States. Ecological Economics, 52:273-288.

7. Bruce A. Stein, 2002. States of the Union: Ranking America's Biodiversity. Arlington, Virginia: NatureServe, 25 pp.

8. Minnesota Department of Natural Resources, 2012. Cypripedium candidum Small White Lady's Slipper. http://www.dnr.state.mn.us/rsg/profile.html?action=elementDetail&selectedElement=PMORCOQ050

9. William R. Thomas, J.W. Stringer, T.E. Conners, D.B. Hill, and T.G. Barnes, 2006. Kentucky Forest Fact Sheet. U.K. Cooperative Extension Publication FOR 53, 2 pp.

10. Kentucky Tourism, Arts, and Heritage Cabinet report, 2012. Economic Impact of Kentucky's Travel and Tourism Industry - 2010 and 2011, 10 pp.

11. U.S. Department of the Interior, Fish and Wildlife Service, and U.S. Department of Commerce, U.S. Census Bureau, 2006 National Survey of Fishing, Hunting, and Wildlife-Associated Recreation, Kentucky, 91 pp.

12. Kentucky Agricultural Statistics 2009-2010 Bulletin, http://www.nass.usda.gov/ky.

13. U.S. Cancer Statistics Working Group. United States Cancer Statistics: 1999–2008 Incidence and Mortality Web-based Report. Atlanta (GA): Department of Health and Human Services, Centers for Disease Control and Prevention, and National Cancer Institute; 2012. Available at: http://www.cdc.gov/uscs.

14. E Ulsperger, 1999. A Cost-Comparison Study of Gemcitabine Versus Cisplatin + Etoposide in Non Small Cell Lung Cancer (NSCLC) (Meeting abstract 1999 ASCO Annual Meeting).

15. Pearce, D. and S. Puroshothaman, 1998. Protecting Biological Diversity: The Economic Value of Pharmaceutical Plants in T. Swanson (ed.) Intellectual Property Rights and Biodiversity Conservation: An interdisciplinary analysis of the values of medicinal plants. Cambridge Univ. Press.

16. FAO, 1999. Women: users, preservers and managers of agrobiodiversity (available at www.fao.org/FOCUS/E/Women/Biodiv-e.htm).

17. Noncitrus Fruits and Nuts 2010 Preliminary Summary (January 2011) 3 USDA, National Agricultural Statistics Service.

18. Robert Costanza, R. d'Arge, R. de Groot§, S. Farberk, M. Grasso, Bruce Hannon, K. Limburg, S. Naeem, R. O'Neill, J. Paruelo, R. Raskin, P. Suttonkk, M. van den Belt, 1997. The value of the world's ecosystem services and natural capital. Nature 387: 253-260.

Index

A
acidic mesophytic 104
acidic xeric woodlands 37
acid mesophytic forest 52
Adkisson Greenbelt Trail 19
agave 132, 133
agrimony 63
alfalfa 84
Allegheny spurge 37, 42, 85
Allegheny wood rat 133
Allen County, Kentucky 39
alligator gar 26
alumroot 27, 126
amaranth 77
American Bald Eagle 16
American basswood 22, 24, 38, 39, 40, 44, 45, 69, 85, 89, 91, 92, 93, 112, 113, 123, 133
American beech 22, 24, 27, 34, 36, 37, 39, 42, 49, 52, 55, 56, 61, 64, 68, 69, 70, 76, 79, 82, 84, 85, 87, 90, 91, 92, 94, 96, 99, 100, 101, 102, 104, 111, 112, 114, 123, 126, 128, 131, 133, 137
American bison 29
American bladdernut 45, 85, 130
American chestnut 65, 66, 75, 76
American columbo 87
American elderberry 60
American elm 30, 40, 42, 43, 45, 61, 77, 81, 87, 91, 97, 99, 102, 112, 113, 114, 122, 125, 126, 130, 133, 138, 139
American frog's bit 127
American golden saxifrage 69
American holly 27, 49, 64, 85, 119, 120
American hop hornbeam 61, 72, 99
American hornbeam 28, 39, 43, 47, 61, 78, 79, 99, 101, 119, 129, 130
American persimmon 30
American plum 60
American snowbell 87
American sycamore 89
American toads 122
American water willow 120
amphibian 32, 38, 43, 49, 60, 62, 65, 70, 73, 76, 77, 89, 92, 93, 97, 100, 102, 103, 104, 105, 107, 108, 112, 113, 117, 119, 122, 123, 128, 129, 131, 137, 139
amphipod 67
anglepod milkvine 139
aphid 15
Appalachian acid seep 27, 56
Appalachian bugbane 87, 101
Appalachian dry 24
Appalachian mesophytic forest 27, 37, 66, 119
Appalachian pine oak 56, 119
Appalachian rosinweed 21
Appalachian sandwort 92
Appalachian sedge 123
Appalachian stitchwort 120
Appalachian subxeric forest 37, 120
Apple Valley Glades 20
Archer-Benge State Nature Preserve 21
Archer, Hugh 21
arctic reedgrass 64
aromatic sumac 132
arrowhead 79
arrowwood viburnum 130
ash 104
asters 133
autumn olive 74, 76, 98, 114, 131
awns 30
azaleas 110

B
baby blue-eyes 129
backwater sloughs 139
Bad Branch State Nature Preserve 24
Bailey's sedge 119
Baker Natural Area 25
Baker, Terrell "Red" 5
bald cypress 81, 87
bald eagle 22, 31, 103
Ballard County, Kentucky 23, 31
Baltimore checkerspot 11, 92
baneberry 27, 70, 129
barnyard grass 105
Barren County, Kentucky 34, 95
Barrens silky aster 73, 84, 128
basket oak 139
basswood 27, 37, 45, 49, 61, 72, 82, 96, 114
bastard toad flax 20, 32
bat 65, 72, 88, 95, 135
Bayou clubtail 129
bedrock 20, 21
bedstraw 63
bee balm 93
beech 91, 104, 139
beech-buckeye 82
Beech forests 82
beech-maple coves 104
beech-white oak 82
beefsteak 9
beggar's tick 87
Bell County, Kentucky 110
bellwort 39, 84
Benge, Dennis 21
bent 84
bergamot 74, 133
Berry, Wendell 6
Bickford, James 69
big bluestem 93, 121, 126
big brown bats 131
big-eared bat 83, 139
big-leaf magnolia 49, 69, 120, 123
Big Rivers Wildlife Management Area and State Forest 26
big shellbark 61
bird 32, 38, 43, 49, 60, 62, 70, 73, 76, 77, 81, 83, 88, 89, 92, 93, 97, 102, 104, 105, 107, 108, 112, 113, 117, 119, 123, 126, 128, 129, 131, 133, 138, 139
bird's foot violet 87, 132
bird-voiced tree frog 97, 127
bishop's cap 27, 34
bitternut 27, 101, 113
bitternut hickory/hickories 32, 43, 44, 45, 49, 52, 60, 61, 69, 76, 78, 84, 87, 93, 98, 99, 121, 125, 129
blackberry/blackberries 34, 60, 66, 74, 134
black birch 120
black cherry 19, 30, 32, 37, 43, 45, 47, 49, 61, 74, 79, 81, 86, 88, 89, 91, 98, 99, 100, 111, 112, 113, 121, 126, 130, 139
black chestnut 84
black cohosh 92
black ducks 81
black-eyed susan 25, 73, 93
black gum 27, 28, 47, 55, 56, 64, 69, 73, 75, 79, 81, 82, 91, 96, 99, 100, 104, 120, 129, 131, 137, 138, 139
blackhaw/black haw 84, 116
black huckleberry 49, 83
blackjack oak 26, 30, 47, 70, 86, 121
black locust 43, 63, 75, 76, 79, 89, 91, 98, 111, 114, 131, 139
black maple 43, 60, 61, 114
black oak 20, 24, 27, 30, 40, 42, 43, 49, 54, 56, 66, 70, 72, 79, 80, 82, 84, 86, 88, 90, 96, 100, 101, 108, 110, 120, 128, 130, 131, 133, 137, 139
Blackside 21
blackside dace 24, 27
black snake root 102
blacktail redhorse 127
black-throated green warblers 83
black tupelo 92
black walnut 30, 32, 37, 38, 43, 44, 45, 52, 60, 61, 63, 68, 73, 74, 77, 78, 79, 81, 82, 83, 86, 87, 88, 89, 91, 93, 98, 99, 101, 102, 107, 111, 112, 113, 120, 125, 126, 129, 130, 131, 133, 138, 139
black warblers 83
black willow 44, 61, 122, 129, 134, 139
bladdernut 38, 43, 52, 61, 72, 114, 126, 128, 133
Blanton Forest State Nature Preserve 27
blazingstar 20, 46, 73, 128
bleufer 97
blind crayfish 88
Blood River crayfish 28
Blood River State Nature Preserve 28
bloodroot 14, 27, 37, 40, 42, 61, 69, 72, 84, 85, 89, 113, 116, 123, 126, 130, 139
blue ash 20, 32, 38, 40, 43, 44, 45, 52, 60, 61, 72, 73, 74, 85, 89, 116, 131, 133
blue beech 73
blueberry/blueberries 27, 47, 56, 65, 70, 79, 92, 102, 108, 110, 120, 121, 123
blue cohosh 27, 70, 84, 114
bluecurls 70
blue-eyed Mary 22, 113, 116, 117, 139
bluegrass 47, 74, 108, 116
blue-green algae 54
blue heron rookery 114
blue jasmine leatherflower 81
Blue Licks Battlefield State Park 30
Blue Licks State Park 29
blue lobelia 62
blue mud plantain 81
blue phlox 34, 36, 39, 42, 73, 84, 116, 126, 130
blue scorpion weed 129
blue star 87
bluestem 25, 32, 33, 46, 47, 65, 73, 87, 118, 121, 128, 132
blue sucker 63
bluets 84, 129
blue violet 52
Blue-winged warbler 37
bluntface shiner 127
Boatwright Wildlife Management Area 23, 31
bobcat 7
boneset 79
Boone Cliffs 61
Boone County, Kentucky 61
Boone, Daniel 29, 96, 108, 109, 119, 136
bottomland hardwood forest system 23
Bouteloua Barrens State Nature Preserve 32
Bouteloua curtipendula 32
boxelder/box elder 38, 44, 45, 52, 61, 63, 68, 72, 74, 77, 78, 87, 89, 97, 98, 105, 111, 112, 114, 116, 126, 129, 130, 133, 138, 139
box huckleberry 49, 119
Boyle County, Kentucky 106
bracken 27
bracken fern 65
bracted water willow 87
Bradbury's bee balm 86
Bragg, Braxton 115
Braun, Lucy 24, 29, 69, 125
Braun's rock cress 125
Breckinridge County, Kentucky 139
Breckinridge County Wildlife Education Park 33
briers 34
Brigadoon State Nature Preserve 34
brighteye darter 127
Broke Leg Falls 35
brook lamprey 127
brook saxifrage 92
Brooks, Thomas B. 41
broomsedge 30, 46, 47, 64, 84, 104, 105
Brown Bat 57
brown madtom 127
Buck Creek Nature Preserve 36
buckeye 38, 131
Buckeye butterflies 118
Buckley's goldenrod 87
buckwheat vine 81, 87
buffalo-nut 49
bugleweed 63, 120
Bullard, Steve 5
Bullitt County, Kentucky 20, 70, 79
bull thistle 77
bulrush 96
bur 60, 61, 78, 126
bur-cucumber 139
burdock 77
Burnett Watershed and Wildlife Conservation Area 37
burning bush 112
bur oak 26, 32, 44, 60, 73, 107
burr cucumber 81
bush 74, 131
bush clover 32, 64
bush honeysuckle 9, 61, 63, 112, 114
bushy broomsedge 64
Butler's quillwort 54
buttercup 87
butterflies 32, 60, 73, 89, 92, 119
butterfly milkweed 60, 73
butterfly pea 65, 79
button 25
button blazingstar 132, 133
buttonbush 45, 61, 87, 97, 104, 139
buttonweed 93, 133, 139

C
cabbage butterfly 12
Cajun dwarf crayfish 97
calcareous forest 32
calcareous mesophytic 37, 39, 43, 52
calcareous sub-xeric forest 37
Caldwell County, Kentucky 104
callary pear 105
Calloway County, Kentucky 28
camellia 49
Camp Nelson Civil War Heritage Park 38
Canada burnet 24
Canada clearweed 117
Canada Frostweed 65, 66
Canada goldenrod 47
Canada goose 103
Canada lily 27, 96, 120
Canada milk vetch 87
Canada white violet 130
canebreaks 126
cardinal 7, 11
cardinal flower 79, 104, 120
Carlisle County, Kentucky 97
Carolina buckthorn 20, 32, 39, 54, 60, 72, 79, 80, 83, 85, 101, 116, 121, 128, 137
Carolina Chickadees 63
Carolina delphinium 25
Carolina fanwort 23
Carolina puccoon 116
Carolina snailseed 81
Carolina willow 77
Carpenter Cave 39
Carter Caves State Resort Park 40, 131
Carter County, Kentucky 40, 100, 131
catspaw 51, 115
cattails 79
cave beetle 21, 48
cave crayfish 48
cave cricket 48, 88
cavefish 67
cave shrimp 132
Cayaponia 87
cedar 113, 121, 131
cedar-oak woodlands 20
cedar sedge 47
celandine poppy 34
cerulean 81
Cerulean warbler 37
chain pickerel 97, 129
cherrybark oak 26, 81, 87, 97, 105
chestnut 24, 47, 49, 56, 61, 75, 76
chestnut blight 9
chestnut oak 27, 46, 65, 66, 68, 69, 70, 75, 79, 82, 91, 92, 96, 100, 101, 102, 108, 110, 120, 121, 123, 128, 131, 133
chestnut sedge 25
chickweed 9, 30, 43, 77, 91, 125
Chinese yam 9
chinquapin 43, 54, 74, 84, 86, 87
chinquapin oak 20, 30, 32, 38, 39, 40, 42, 43, 45, 46, 48, 52, 60, 63, 72, 73, 78, 81, 84, 86, 88, 89, 90, 93, 98, 99, 111, 113, 114, 116, 120, 121, 125, 128, 131, 133
Christian County, Kentucky 101, 104
Christmas fern 20, 52, 68, 104, 119, 123
cinereous shrew 24, 27
cinnamon 27, 56
cinnamon chain ferns 28
cinnamon fern 27, 49, 56, 96, 120
Civil War Earthen Works 41
Clark County, Kentucky 18, 41, 89
Clark, George Rogers 136
Clark, Thomas D. 89
Clay Hill Memorial Forest 42
Clay Wildlife Management Area 43
Clear Creek Park Greenway 44
cleft phlox 72
Clematis pitcheri 87
cliff 120
cliffbrake ferns 85
cliff-melic grass 38
climbing dogbane 87
climbing fern 120
Clinton's lily 92
clover 84
clubshell 51, 115, 126, 132
coastal plain sedge 129
columbine 61, 73, 89, 126
Combs, Bert T. 35
common groundsel 63
common rush 77
coneflower 25
copepod 67
copperbelly 26
copperbelly watersnake 98, 103
coral berry/coralberry 52, 74, 77, 79, 93
corn salad 63
Cornwallis 29
Costanza, R. 15
cottonwood 19, 23, 45, 63, 81, 122, 129, 130
Cove Springs Nature Preserve 45
crawdad 11
Crawe's sedge 20, 32, 73, 128
crayfish 11
crested coralroot orchid 87
crinkled hairgrass 92, 123
Crittenden County, Kentucky 26
Crooked Creek Barrens 46
crossvine 81
croton 93
crown vetch 74
Crumps Cave Education and Research Preserve 48
crustaceans 97
cucumber 82, 92, 120
cucumber magnolia 69
cucumber tree 27, 37, 49, 56, 66, 75, 76, 85, 129
Cumberland Arrow Darter 21, 92
Cumberland Bean 36
Cumberland County, Kentucky 91
Cumberland Darter 11, 21
Cumberland elktoe 21
Cumberland Falls 7
Cumberland Falls State Resort Park 49
Cumberland Gap National Historical Park 11
Cumberland Papershell 21
cupseed 87
Curtis' goldenrod 24, 75, 92, 123
cutleaf coneflower 116
cut-leaf prairie dock 25
cut-leaf toothwort 74, 89
cypress minnow 23, 129
Cypress trees 97, 129
cypress-tupelo swamp 23

D
damselfly 127
Daniel Boone National Forest 11, 49
Daviess County 19, 138
Davis Bend Watershed and Wildlife Conservation Area 51
dead wood 80
deer 112
degrees 30
Department of Fish and Wildlife Resources 8
Department of Parks 8
devil's walking stick 30
Diana fritillary 92
Dietz, Joe 5, 78, 135
Dinsmore Woods 61
dittany 86, 87, 116
Division of Forestry 8
Division of Water 140
dogwood 27, 30, 32, 37, 39, 47, 57, 70, 79, 84, 120, 126, 128
dollar sunfish 97, 127, 129
doll's eyes 42, 52, 61
Dorman, Tom 130
downslope 119
Downy 72
downy alumroot 104
downy arrowwood 40
downy rattlesnake orchid 120
downy rattlesnake plantain 123
downy serviceberry 79, 82, 92, 96, 120
downy viburnum 85
dragonflies 92
dropseed 20, 32, 54, 73, 84, 128, 132
dry calcareous forest 52
Dry Fork Gorge 52
dry sandstone cliff 37
Duckweed 78
dutchman's breeches 34, 44, 73, 113, 130
dward crested iris 85
dwarf blazing star 86
dwarf crested iris 27, 34, 69, 79, 84, 100
dwarf dandelion 87
dwarf hackberry 93
dwarf larkspur 63, 73, 84, 126, 130
dwarf sundew 64

E
eagles 16
early saxifrage 89
eastern cottonwood 97
eastern eulophus 54
eastern hemlock 36, 69, 75, 92, 96, 120, 123, 135
eastern hop hornbeam 69
eastern leatherwood 85
eastern lined asters 139
eastern redbud 73, 83, 101
eastern red cedar 34, 88, 101, 111
eastern ribbon snake 10, 127
eastern sand 63
Eastern small footed myotis 92
eastern wahoo 83
eastern whiteflower beard tongue 132
eastern white pine 34
Eastview Barrens State Nature Preserve 53
ebony spleenwort 104
Eggert's sunflower 56, 121, 132
Eggleston's violet 32, 130
egrets 23
elderberry 89
Elliott's broomsedge 84
elm 40, 85, 102
elm-leaf goldenrod 87
emerald ash borers 9
enchanter's nightshade 24, 75
endangered blue-flowered coyote thistle 97
endangered cypress minnow 97
endangered green water snake 97
endemic bottlebrush crayfish 67
endemics 67
Environmental Education and Research Center 80
Envirothon 25
ephiphytic sedge 97
ericaceous shrubs 24
Evans, Mark 21
evening bat 23, 89, 105, 112, 129
eyeless crayfish 67

F
fairy wand 96
fall panicum 105
Falls of the Ohio 29
false aloe 20, 73
false dandelion 139
false foxglove 65
false indigo 139
false nettle 87, 116
false rue anemone 72, 92, 113
false Solomon's seal 27, 47, 126
fanshell 51, 115, 132
farkleberry 39, 49, 86, 87, 104, 128
fat pocketbook mussel 26
fence lizards 73
ferns 27, 75, 120
ferries 41
fescue 74, 77
fetterbush 69
firebelly darter 127
fire pink 61, 89, 126
fish 63, 67, 77, 101, 107, 113, 129, 132
fish crow 97, 129
five lobed cucumber 87
Flat Lick Falls 17
Flat Rock Glade State Nature Preserve 54
flat-topped aster 96
flatwoods 137
flax 86
fleabane 54
Fleming County, Kentucky 43, 102
flowered trillium 52
flowering dogwood 24, 61, 72, 73, 81, 82, 83, 85, 86, 97,

99, 102, 104, 111, 114, 120, 129, 137
flowering spurge 32, 128, 132
fluted kidneyshell 36
foamflower 27, 40, 52, 123
forbs 21
fords 41
forest tickseed 120
Forrest, Nathan Bedford 55
Fort Boonesboro 29
Fort Heiman National Battlefield 55
foxgloves 47
fox grape 84
fragrant sumac 93
Frances Johnson Palk State Nature Preserve 56
Franklin County, Kentucky 45, 74, 114, 116, 125
Fraser's magnolia 24, 75, 92, 123
Fraser's sedge 24, 123
Frasier's magnolia 27, 66, 69
French grass 32, 65, 121
Frenchman's Knob Conservation Area 57
French's shooting star 139
freshwater clam 11
fresh water mussels 15
fringed loosestrife 133
fringe-tree 30
frost aster 105
Fulton County, Kentucky 97
fungi/fungus 12, 15

G

galax 65
garlic mustard 9, 30, 43, 44, 61, 63, 74, 77, 112, 114, 125
garlic mustard winter creeper 63
Garrard County, Kentucky 130
gaura 20, 32
gentian 75, 123
giant cane 79, 87, 101, 129
ginger 114, 116
ginseng 52, 78, 91
glade coneflower 132, 133
glade st. johns wort 132
Glenview Nature Preserve 58
globe beaked rush 64
globe bladderpod 45
gnarled 47
goat's rue 65, 86, 87
goblet asters 139
golden Alexander 60
goldenglow 63
golden ragwort 36, 89
goldenrod 47, 63, 65, 73, 98, 105, 133, 134
goldenseal 20, 61, 87, 91
goldstripe 127
grape 15
grape honeysuckle 89
grasses 79
Graves County, Kentucky 97, 127
gray bat 26, 28, 38, 39, 51, 83, 89, 95, 101, 107, 133, 139
gray coneflower 132, 133
gray goldenrod 32, 93, 128
gray headed coneflower 73, 93
gray tree frog 105
great blue heron rookery 28
Great Blue Herons 114
greater tickseed 133
great laurel 123
Great Plains Ladies Tresse 30
green antelope horn milkweed 32
green ash 19, 28, 38, 45, 78, 81, 87, 97, 98, 102, 107, 111, 129, 133, 134, 139
greenbrier 66, 68, 79, 92, 102
green dragon 73, 129
green frog 122, 126
green milkweed 93
Green River State Forest 59
green tree frog 23, 129, 139
green violet 84, 87
green-winged teal 81
Griffith Woods 60
grizzly bears 16
ground cedar 49
ground cover 65
groundnut 81
gulf darters 127
gull 31
Gunpowder Creek 61

H

hackberry 20, 30, 32, 34, 38, 43, 45, 63, 79, 83, 88, 89, 93, 99, 111, 112, 114, 118, 121, 125, 126, 138, 139
hackberry cedar 30
hairy alumroot 120
hairy false gromwell 32
Hairy fimbristylis 121
hairy lespedeza 32, 128
hairy phlox 50
hairy skullcap 86
hairy sunflower 121, 133
hairy water primrose 64
hairy wood mint 128
harbinger of spring 52
Hardin County, Kentucky 73, 121
Harlan County, Kentucky 6, 27, 65, 69, 75, 92, 110, 123
Harrison County, Kentucky 60
Hart County, Kentucky 51, 67, 115, 132
Hawthorne Crossing Conservation Area 63
hay-scented 104
hazel alder 119, 120
Hazeldell Meadow 64
hazelnut 79
heartleaf 123
heartleaf noseburn 132
hearts-a-burstin' 70
hedge hyssop 120
Heiman, Adolphus 55
hemlock 21, 24, 27, 49, 56, 66, 69, 75, 82, 119, 123
hemlock forest 12
hemlock tree 12, 24
hemlock wooly adelgid 9, 12
henbit 77
Henderson County, Kentucky 22
Henry County, Kentucky 77, 78
Henslow's sparrow 36, 47
hepatica 34, 72, 89, 120
herbaceous 37, 43, 60, 65
heron rookery 22
Hickman County, Kentucky 81, 97, 129
hickory/hickories 21, 23, 25, 40, 42, 55, 57, 83, 90, 91, 94, 100, 101, 111, 131
hickory trees 60
Hidden River Cave 67
highbush 70
highbush blueberry 49, 104
High View Hill 68
Hi Lewis Pine Barrens State Nature Preserve 65
hillside blueberry 49
hispid false mallow 54
hoary puccoon 20, 73, 84, 128, 132
hog peanut 77, 114, 133
honey locust 43, 63, 76, 79, 89, 105, 111
honeysuckle 63, 77, 89
hooded warbler 37, 83
hop hornbeam/hophornbeam 47, 52, 73, 79, 86, 101, 114, 120, 126, 128, 133
Hopkins County, Kentucky 104
hornbeam 70, 98, 133
horse mint 87
horses 19
huckleberries 24, 27, 56, 92, 108, 110, 120
hummingbird 7
hydrangea 27, 77, 98, 114

I

Illinois pondweed 37
Indiana bat 21, 26, 51, 57, 65, 91, 101, 107, 129, 131, 135, 139
Indian cucumber 92
Indiangrass 25, 32, 33, 65, 73, 87, 93, 105, 126, 128, 132
Indian paintbrush 47
Indian pink 87
Indian tobacco 92
indigo bush 133
insects 65
interior least tern 26
ironweed 44, 94, 111
ironwood 70, 94, 102, 120, 131
isopod 67, 69

J

jack-in-the-pulpit 34, 40, 42, 52, 70, 79, 84, 91, 114, 120, 126, 129, 130, 139
Jackson County, Kentucky 17
Jacob's ladder 42, 61, 79, 84
James E. Bickford State Nature Preserve 69
Japanese barberry 112
Japanese chaff flower 9
Japanese grass 63
Japanese honeysuckle 9, 30, 43, 47, 74, 77, 102, 131
Japanese hops 63, 77
Japanese knotweed 9
Japanese stilt grass 12, 43, 77, 102, 114, 131
Jefferson County, Kentucky 7, 20, 70, 107, 111
Jefferson Memorial Forest 70
Jefferson's salamanders 122
Jerusalem artichoke 139
Jessamine County, Kentucky 72, 130
Jessamine Creek Nature Preserve 72
jewelweed 114
Jim Scudder State Nature Preserve 73
joe pye weed 79
John James Audubon State Park 22
johnson grass 9, 77
jointed rush 123
Jones, Morgan 5
Julian Savanna 74
Juneberry 86

K

KDFWR 103
Kentenia State Forest 75
Kenton County, Kentucky 94
Kentucky coffeetree 60, 61, 81
Kentucky Department of Fish and Wildlife Resources 11, 81, 97
Kentucky Department of Parks 6, 49, 106
Kentucky Division of Forestry 140
Kentucky Division of Water Wild Rivers Program 49
Kentucky Glade Cress 20
Kentucky lady slipper 119, 135
Kentucky Natural Lands Trust 21, 140
Kentucky Ridge State Forest and Wildlife Management Area 76
Kentucky River Wildlife Management Area 77
Kentucky State Nature Preserve 5, 11, 23, 39, 46
Kentucky State University Environmental Education and Research Center 78
Kentucky warbler 37, 73, 83
Kentucky Wild Rivers program 8
Kentucky yellow wood 130
kidney leaf tway-blade 24
kingnut hickory 81, 87
Kirkland's snake 127
Knobs State Forest 79
KSNPC 23, 32, 66, 73, 129

L

lake chubsucker 23, 97
lanceleaf buckthorn 89
large buttonweed 87
large-flowered bellwort 69, 123
large-flowered trillium 69, 92, 123
LaRue County, Kentucky 128
LaRue Environmental Education and Research Center 80
late purple aster 89
laurel 92
Laurel County, Kentucky 119, 134
Laurel Fork 21
lavender waterleaf 113
leaf beetle 78
leaf pine 49
leaf rhododendron 12, 27
leatherwood 52
LeClerc, Gilbert 57
leeks 91
Leonard's skullcap 20
Leopold, Aldo 6
lesser celandine 112
lesser siren 127
Letcher County, Kentucky 24, 82, 110
Letourneau Woods 81
Lewis County, Kentucky 46
lichen 12, 27, 54, 75, 92
Lilley Cornett Woods 82
Lily Mountain Nature Preserve 83
limber honeysuckle 40
limestone 54, 61
limestone bedrock 25
limestone calamint 78
limestone fameflower 54
limestone glades 25, 29, 30
Lincoln, Abraham 84
Lincoln Boyhood Home National Historic Site 84
Lincoln County, Kentucky 32, 136
little bluestem 20, 65, 87, 93, 126, 132
little brown bats 131
little ladies tresses 70
Little South Fork 85
liverworts 65
Livingston County, Kentucky 8, 86
Livingston County Natural Areas 86
Livingston County Wildlife Management Area 8
lizard tail 77
lobed hepatica 85
lobed violet 86
loblolly pine 99, 132
Loesel's twayblade 69, 92
Logan County, Kentucky 25
longclaw crayfish 92
Long leaf rhododendron 76
long-spurred violets 120
Lost River Cave 88
Louisiana waterthrush 37
Louv, Richard 16
lovegrass 52
low bush blueberry 70
Lower Howards Creek 18
Lower Howard's Creek Nature and Heritage Preserve 89
Lucy Braun's Rock cress 125
Luna moths 50

M

magnolia 35, 119
maidenhair-fern 51
maidenhair spleenwort ferns 27
Mallard ducks 81
mallards 81
mammal 32, 38, 43, 49, 60, 62, 65, 70, 73, 76, 77, 89, 92, 93, 97, 102, 104, 105, 107, 108, 112, 117, 123, 128, 129, 131, 133, 138, 139
Mammoth Cave National Park 11, 52
mannagrass 96
maple 23, 80, 118
maple leaf viburnum 27, 37, 49, 69, 70, 96, 120
maple tree 38
marginal shield fern 86
marginal wood fern 104
Marion County, Kentucky 90
Marion County Wildlife Management Area and State Forest 90
Marrowbone State Forest 91
marsh blue violet 77, 120
Martin, Bill 5
Martins Fork of the Cumberland River State Natural Area 92
Martin, William H. 4
Maryland golden aster 65
Masked shrew 69
mastodons 29
matriarch's grape fern 24
mayapple 37, 39, 60, 74, 85
McAlpin Dam 29
McCoy's blue hole 132
McCracken County, Kentucky 105
McCreary County, Kentucky 37, 49, 85
meadow beauty 27
meadow pink 79
meadow selaginella 49
Menifee County, Kentucky 35
mesic bluegrass 61
mesic calcareous 112
mesic ravines 56
mesic/wet sandstone cliff 37
mesophytic 24
Metcalfe County, Kentucky 91
Miami mist 74
Michaux's bluets 21
Michaux's saxifrage 24
millipede 69
mimic shiner 63
Mississippi kite 97, 129
Missouri arrow-wood 89
mock bishop's weed 28
mockernut 70, 84, 99
mockernut hickories 56, 72, 96, 131, 139
mockernut hickory 39, 77, 79, 82, 85, 102, 104, 108, 113, 119, 121
Mock orange 85
monkey faced orchid 56
monkey flower 79
Monroe County, Kentucky 99
moonseed vine 81
Morgan Conservation Park 93
Morgan, John Hunt 126
Morning View Conservation Area 94
moss 27, 65, 75, 92, 108
moth 32, 56, 60, 89, 133
mountain camellia 50, 119
mountain holly 49
mountain Indian-physic 50
mountain laurel 27, 49, 65, 70, 79, 92, 96, 108, 110, 120, 123
mountain lover 72
mountain midget crayfish 92
mountain spleenwort 27, 123
mouse ear chickweed 79
mud glyphs 48
mudminnow 97, 127
mud snake 28
mugwort 139
Muhlenberg County, Kentucky 103
Mulkey, John 99
Mulkey, Philip 99
multiflora rose 9, 43, 63, 74, 76, 102, 112, 131
muskie 63
musk thistle 9, 30, 74
mussel 11, 21, 36, 37, 51, 63, 67, 107, 115, 119, 126, 132, 135
Mutter's Cave 95

N

naked tick trefoil 65
narrow-leafed sundrops 64
narrow leaf evening-primrose 121
narrowleaf silkgrass 65
narrow leaf vervain 93
Natural Bridge State Resort Park 96
Nature Preserves Commission 8, 140
netted chain ferns 28
New England aster 93
New Jersey tea 96
New York fern 27, 49
Nicholas County, Kentucky 30, 43
nodding 113
nodding onion 132
Nodding rattlesnake root 89
nodding thistle 77
nodding trillium 114
Northern fence lizard 41
northern hackberry 77
northern leopard frogs 77
northern red oak 27, 34, 35, 38, 39, 40, 43, 44, 45, 49, 52, 56, 66, 70, 72, 73, 75, 76, 78, 79, 82, 84, 85, 87, 89, 90, 91, 92, 96, 98, 100, 101, 104, 108, 114, 116, 119, 120, 123, 126, 128, 129, 130, 131, 138, 139
northern rifleshell 51, 115, 132
northern spicebush 83
Northern White Cedar 36
noseburn 52
Nutall's oak 28

O

oak 21, 22, 23, 25, 37, 57, 68, 82, 90, 94, 100, 104, 131
oak-hickory 104, 108
Obion Creek State Nature Preserve 97
Obion Creek Wildlife Management Area 81
Ocoone bells 96
Ohio buckeye 32, 38, 42, 43, 44, 45, 60, 61, 63, 72, 73, 78, 91, 113, 114, 116, 125, 126, 130, 133
Ohio County, Kentucky 98, 103
Ohio County Park and Natural Area 98
old-field aster 139
Oldham County, Kentucky 93, 112
Old Mulkey Meeting House 99
Olive Hill Reservoir Preservation 100
Olympia marble butterfly 133
orange coneflower 32
orange grass 86
orchard grass 47, 63, 84
orchids 119
oriental bittersweet 112
osage orange 63, 80, 88, 89, 111, 114
Outer Bluegrass Bird Conservation Ecoregion 90
ovenbird 37, 73, 83
overcup oak 81, 97
Overton Cave Conservation Easement 101
Owen County, Kentucky 77

P

paddlefish 63
painted trillium 24, 92
pale corydalis 21
pale indian plantain 87
pale jewelweed 120
pale mandarin 123
pale purple coneflower 20, 73
pale spiked lobelia 73
palezone shiner 37
Park Lake Mountain Nature Preserve 102
partridge berry 27, 119, 123
Passion flower 95
pasture rose 60
patriarch trees 60
pawpaw/paw paw 52, 60, 61, 68, 70, 78, 79, 80, 81, 83, 89, 98, 99, 101, 102, 114, 120, 125, 128, 129, 130, 133, 137
Peabody WMA 103
peavine 52
pecan 81, 87, 126
pencil flower 121
Pennington, Hannah Boone 99
Pennyrile State Forest 104
Pennyrile State Resort Park 104
pennyroyal 93, 97
pepper bush 27
peppervine 81
perfoliate bellwort 92, 129
Perkins Creek Nature Preserve 105
Perryville Battlefield State Historic Site 106
persimmon 20, 81, 89, 98, 128
Peterson 107
phacelia 104
phagnum moss 28
phlox 63, 114
piedmont azalea 28
pigeons 16
pignut 70, 72, 82, 87, 96, 99, 121, 137
pignut hickory 20, 27, 28, 30, 39, 40, 46, 47, 49, 63, 66, 69, 73, 78, 79, 82, 84, 86, 92, 100, 101, 102, 104, 108, 120, 123, 128, 139
Pilot Knob State Nature Preserve 108, 109
pine 66, 75, 79, 81, 87
Pine Mountain State Scenic Trail 110
pine-oak 24, 27, 66, 108
pink lady slipper 75
pink mucket 51, 115
pink thoroughwort 87
pinnatifid spleenwort 86
pin oak 44, 61, 64, 87, 105, 122, 129, 134
Pinxter-flower azaleas 100
piping plover 26
pitch 27, 49, 56, 65, 92, 110, 120
pitch pine 21, 27, 75, 123
planetree 81
plumleaf viburnum 43
pocketbook 132
poison hemlock 74, 77
poison ivy 77, 81
polar bears 16
polypody fern 27, 86
pondweed 85
Pope Lick Park 111
possum haw 97, 129
possum haw viburnum 28
post-black jack oak barrens 29
post oak 20, 32, 46, 49, 54, 56, 72, 79, 86, 99, 105, 108, 121, 128
post oak mockernut 128
poverty grass 20, 86
poverty oak grass 86
Powell County, Kentucky 96, 108
prairie dock 46, 128
prairie gentian 121
prairie grasses 25
prairie heart-leaf aster 50
prairie phlox 73
prairie redroot 85
prairie tea 20, 32, 132
Price's potato bean 87
prickly ash 20, 30
prickly bog sedge 28
prickly pear cactus 25, 54, 84, 86, 132
princess tree 112
privet 9, 43, 77, 112
prothonotary 81
Pulaski County, Kentucky 36, 56, 135
purple daisy 87
purple Lilliput 36
purple meadow rue 120
purple oatgrass 72, 130
purple phacelia 39, 72, 113
purple prairie clover 25
purple top 30, 105
purple wake robins 69
Putney Pond and Woodlands Natural Area 112
pyramid pigtoe 132

Q

Queen Anne's lace 9, 30, 63, 74

R

Rafinesque's big-eared bat 37, 120
rainbow darters 11
rare orchids 16
rare vine 87
rattlesnake master 133
rattlesnake root 78
Raven Run Nature Sanctuary 113
ravines 27
ravine salamanders 122
recurved trillium 138, 139
red ash 61
red-backed vole 24, 27
red buckeye 105
redbud 13, 20, 30, 32, 49, 52, 57, 61, 72, 79, 85, 86, 93, 99, 104, 114, 116, 128
red cedar 20, 30, 32, 38, 46, 47, 54, 63, 71, 72, 73, 78, 79, 80, 84, 85, 86, 89, 91, 93, 94, 99, 101, 104, 111, 114, 116, 121, 128, 131, 132
red cloves 63
red eared slider 26
red elm 89, 99
red eyed vireo 73
red hickory 82
red maple 21, 23, 24, 27, 28, 34, 39, 43, 47, 49, 56, 61, 64, 66, 69, 71, 75, 76, 79, 81, 82, 90, 91, 92, 96, 97, 98, 99, 100, 102, 104, 105, 108, 110, 111, 119, 120, 123, 130, 131, 134, 137
red mulberry 68, 81, 89
red oak 42, 55, 81, 91, 93, 133
red-post oak 54
Red Shoulder hawks 26
redside dace 63
redspotted sunfish 127
red sundew 64
Red-twig doghobble 24
reed canary grass 63
Renfro, John 34
Renfro, Louis 49
reptile 32, 38, 43, 49, 60, 62, 65, 70, 73, 76, 77, 89, 92, 93, 97, 102, 103, 104, 105, 107, 108, 112, 113, 117, 123, 128, 129, 131, 139
rhododendron 21, 69, 75, 120
ribbon snake 97
rice cut grass 87
rice grass 133
rich spring wildflower 73
rigid goldenrod 128
ring pink 51, 115, 132
ringseed rush 20, 121
riparian 37, 52, 68
riparian vegetation 114
riverbank goldenrod 139
river birch 23, 97, 98, 105
River Cliffs State Nature Preserves 114
river oats 104, 120, 133
Robertson County, Kentucky 30
robin 12
Rockcress Hills State Nature Preserve 117
Rockcress Hills State Nature Preserves 116
rock elm 38, 72
rock harlequin 24, 69, 92, 123
rockhouse alumroot 75
rock polypody ferns 123
rocky glades 121
rosebay rhododendron 24
rosepink 20
rose turtlehead 97, 127
rosinweed 32
rough leaf dogwood 74, 93, 116
rough-leaf dogwood 30
rough pigtoe 51, 115, 132
round-leaf catchfly 75, 120
roundleaf greenbrier 81, 116
roundleaf violets 120
roundseed St. John's wort 73
royal catchfly 132
royal chain ferns 28
royal fern 49, 56, 96
royal princess tree 9
rue 72, 113
rue anemone 20, 34, 42, 89, 91
running buffalo clover 89
rushes 49, 63, 64, 79
Rush Island Watershed and Wildlife Conservation Area 115
rusty blackhaw 30, 32, 85, 86, 101, 116

S

Sable clubtail 92
salamander 28
salamander fauna 11
sandbar 139
sand grape 14, 85, 135
sand hill crane 13
sandwort 132
sassafras 20, 24, 30, 34, 42, 47, 56, 61, 66, 68, 79, 89, 91, 92, 96, 98, 100, 101, 104, 110, 120, 121, 123, 126, 128, 129, 138, 139
scarlet 27, 49, 56, 63, 75, 76
scarlet Indian paintbrush 47, 128
scarlet oak 24, 46, 47, 55, 64, 65, 66, 70, 79, 82, 90, 92, 96, 100, 101, 102, 104, 108, 110, 120, 121, 123, 139
Scarlet red blueberries 24
scattered cherry bark oak 98
scholarly cave beetle 69
Scorpions 73
scrambled eggs 79
sedge 49, 62, 63, 64, 68, 79, 84, 87, 96, 102, 120, 127, 133
sedge wrens 36
sedum 20
sensitive fern 79, 104
sericea lespedeza 102, 131
serviceberry 20, 24, 27, 49, 83, 104, 110, 123
sessile trillium 44, 52, 60, 72, 73, 74, 84, 89, 91, 104, 113, 126
shadow darter 92
shagbark 20, 44, 60, 61, 72, 78, 99
shagbark hickory 27, 30, 42, 43, 47, 52, 73, 79, 84, 86, 87, 98, 100, 105, 108, 118, 121, 126, 128, 130, 131, 133, 139
sharp lobed hepatica 37
sharpnose darters 63
sharp-shinned hawk 96
Shawnee darter 101
Shawnee National Forest 26
sheep 74
sheepnose 51, 115
Shelby County, Kentucky 44
Shelby County Parks and Recreation Department 44
Shelby Trails Park Annex 118
shellbark hickory 43, 56, 60, 78, 129, 137
shingle oak 30, 72, 100
shining bedstraw 87
shining ladies-tresses 85
shooting star 40, 52, 54, 84, 86, 128
shortleaf 27, 56
short-leaf pine 65, 96, 110, 120
shortleaf skeleton grass 64
Short's goldenrod 29, 30
Short's Goldenrod State Nature Preserve 29
showy gentian 24
showy lady slipper orchid 132
Showy orchis 124
shrimp 67
shrimp crayfish 129
shrub 43, 60, 74, 104, 120
Shumard 30, 38, 78, 86, 87, 111, 113, 114, 130
Shumard oak 32, 38, 43, 52, 60, 61, 68, 81, 111, 133
side-oats grama 32, 47
silkgrass 65
silky 120
silky dogwood 38
silky lespedeza 9, 98, 104
silky willow 96
silphiums 73
siltstone-shale glade 90
silverling 92
silver maple 19, 44, 45, 63, 68, 72, 77, 78, 81, 87, 97, 107, 111, 114, 116, 122, 126, 129, 130, 133, 134, 139
Simpson County, Kentucky 54
Sinking Creek 119
slender blazingstar 47
slender heliotrope 25
slender leaf false foxglove 121
slender lespedeza 32
slender madtom 63
slender mountain mint 121
slippery elm 20, 30, 39, 45, 52, 61, 63, 78, 79, 84, 85, 99, 101, 112, 116, 131
small footed myotis 65
small horse gentian 87
small skullcap 121
Small sundrops 24
small yellow lady slipper 75
smart weeds 133
Smith Watershed and Wildlife Conservation Area 120
smooth aster 47
smooth azalea 119
smooth brome 63
smooth phlox 121
smooth sumac 84
smooth wild licorice 86
Snow geese 31
snow melanthera 23
snow squarestem 81
snow trillium 72
soft-leaf arrowwood 72
Solomon and false Solomon's seal 91
Solomon's seal 20, 70, 73, 79
songbirds 106, 136
sourwood 24, 39, 56, 70, 82, 91, 92, 96, 100, 104, 108, 110, 120, 123, 128
southeastern myotis bats 101
southern Appalachian 24
southern basswood 108
southern blackhaw 93, 132
southern bog clubmoss 123
Southern bog goldenrod 135
southern buckthorn 20, 87
southern club moss 64
southern harebell 92
Southern heartleaf 24
southern painted turtle 97
southern pine beetle 66, 76, 119, 120
southern pines 100
southern red oak 26, 28, 30, 49, 56, 70, 75, 82, 86, 88, 99, 108, 121, 137
southern red trillium 123
southern shagbark hickory 132
southern twayblade 97
Spanish oak 104
speckled wood lily 27, 69, 123
spectaclecase 132
sphagnum mosses 27
spicebush 27, 37, 38, 39, 43, 45, 52, 61, 68, 70, 80, 81, 89, 93, 98, 101, 102, 104, 114, 116, 120, 125, 126, 129, 130, 131, 133
spider lily 87
spiked blazingstar/blazing star 47, 121
spiked gay feather 25
spiked lobelia 47
spikenard 61, 92
spinulose wood fern 27, 75, 84, 96, 97
Sportsman Hill 136
spotted 123
spotted geranium 37
spotted knapweed 63
spreading waterleaf 52
spring beauty 44, 52, 73, 79, 84, 91
spring flora 27
Springhouse Barrens 121
Spring peepers 122
spring wildflower 123
squirrel corn 44, 62, 104, 113
stalked wild petunia 87
St. Andrew's cross 64
St. Anne's Woods and Wetlands Conservation Area 122
star chickweed 36
starhead topminnow 97
starry cleft phlox 130, 132
starry false Solomon's seal 46
Steele's joe-pye-weed 24, 75, 92
steep ravines 27, 56
stemless evening primrose 54
stiff aster 121
stiff dogwood 119
stiff gentian 47
stilt grass 74
stinging nettle 77, 114
St. John's wort 20
stonecrop 39, 61, 79, 89, 139
Stone Mountain Wildlife Management and State Natural Area 123
strawberry bush 137
streambank 52
streambank mock orange 37
stream bank wild rye 77
streamline chub 63
streamside salamanders 122
Strohmeier Hill 125
stunted pines 65
sub-xeric 39
sub-xeric calcareous forest 43
sugarberry 68, 81, 139
sugar maple 20, 22, 27, 32, 34, 38, 39, 40, 41, 42, 43, 44, 45, 47, 49, 52, 61, 63, 69, 70, 72, 73, 75, 76, 77, 78, 80, 81, 82, 84, 85, 86, 87, 90, 91, 92, 93, 94, 96, 98, 99, 100, 101, 102, 104, 111, 112, 113, 116, 120, 123, 125, 126, 128, 130, 131, 133, 138, 139
Sulcate's trillium 91
sumac 34, 65, 98, 102, 121
summer grape 87
sundews 64
sunfish 23
sunflower 25, 73, 77, 121
Svenson's wild rye 38, 45
Swainson's warblers 81
swamp chestnut oak 28, 81, 87, 88, 126, 134
swamp milkweed 62, 63
swamp privet 87, 129
swamp rose 97, 134
swamp white 26
swamp white oak 61, 122
sweet birch 24, 27, 35, 66, 75, 92, 96, 119, 120, 123
sweet buckeye 52, 61
sweet clover 47
sweet fern 135
sweetgum/sweet gum 23, 28, 49, 64, 68, 79, 81, 86, 87, 89, 97, 101, 104, 105, 126, 129, 134, 137, 138, 139
sweet mountain pepperbush 120
sweet pepperbush 24
sweet pignut hickory 70, 108
switchgrass 33, 118
sycamore 13, 19, 23, 38, 39, 43, 44, 45, 61, 63, 68, 72, 77, 78, 79, 81, 86, 87, 88, 97, 98, 99, 101, 102, 104, 105, 111, 112, 114, 116, 119, 122, 126, 129, 130, 131, 133, 134, 138, 139
synandra 61

T

taillight shiner 97, 129
tall coreopsis 47
tall dropseed 30, 121
tall fescue 9, 30, 47, 63, 134
tall goldenrod 60
Tate's Creek, Kentucky 41
Tatum cave beetle 90
Taylor County, Kentucky 126
teaberry 120
teasel 63
Tebbs Bend 126
Tennessee clubshell 36, 37
Tennessee leaf cup 129
Terrapin Creek State Nature Preserve 127
Texas liliput 97
thistles 34
Thompson Creek Glade State Nature Preserve 128
three lined salamander 127
Three Ponds State Nature Preserve 129
three toed amphiuma 97
tickseed 128
tickseed coreopsis 92
tick trefoil 87
tiger spiketail 92
timothy 84
timothy grass 47
tippecanoe 63
toadshade 104
toadshade trillium 129
Tom Dorman State Nature Preserve 130
toothwort 42
trailing arbutus 65, 120
tree-of-heaven 9, 12, 68, 112, 114, 131
tri-colored bats 48, 131
trillium 24, 34, 42
trilobed coneflower 52
trogolbitic invertebrates 67
trout lily 39, 42, 84, 89, 91
trumpet creeper 81
tufted hairgrass 130
tulip tree 21, 22, 24, 27, 30, 34, 35, 39, 40, 42, 43, 49, 52, 56, 61, 66, 68, 69, 70, 75, 76, 78, 79, 80, 82, 84, 87, 88, 89, 90, 91, 92, 96, 97, 98, 99, 100, 101, 102, 104, 105, 108, 116, 119, 120, 123, 128, 129, 131, 133, 137, 138, 139
turtle 26
turtlehead 27
twinleaf/twin leaf 61, 70, 72, 73, 79, 84, 91, 113, 116, 120, 130
twisted post 47
two leaf miterwort 123
Tygarts State Forest 131

U

umbrella magnolia 27, 92, 120, 123
umbrella tree 49, 119
Union County, Kentucky 26
upland boneset 86
upland privet 54
Upper Green River Biological Reserve 132
Uruguayan water primrose 77
U.S. Fish and Wildlife Service 21, 96, 97

V

vacciniums 96
various spurges 93
veined skullcap 139
veiny peavine 83
velvet witchgrass 64
vibrunums 72
viceroy 7
viceroy butterflies 11
violet bush clover 87
violets 63, 123
violet wood sorrel 79, 87
Virginia 21, 24, 29, 49, 75, 110, 132
Virginia blue bells 84
Virginia bluebells 34, 89, 116, 126
Virginia creeper 87
Virginia pine 27, 56, 70, 79, 84, 91, 92, 96, 99, 104, 108, 123, 128, 131
Virginia pines 96
Virginia snakeroot 116
Virginia spiderwort 139
Virginia sweetspire 119, 129
Virginia wildrye 74
Virginia willow 97
Virginia winged rockcress 85

W

wahoo 60, 98
walking fern 85
wall rue 89
walnut 9, 15, 16, 34, 38, 96, 107
Walter's violet 72
Warren County, Kentucky 88
waterfowl 22
water hickory 23
waterleaf 52, 61, 63, 70
water locust 81, 129
water snake 26
water stitchwort 72, 89
water tupelo 28
water willow 133, 139
wavy leaf 73
Wayne County, Kentucky 37
weak stellate sedge 28
Wedekind, Carl 4
Weese, Zeb 5, 21, 26, 37, 57, 83, 103, 115, 118, 122, 135
western false gromwell 85
western mud snake 97, 127
western wood sorrel 52
wet flatwoods 64
white 43, 49, 61
white ash 20, 27, 30, 32, 34, 38, 39, 40, 43, 44, 45, 47, 52, 55, 61, 63, 68, 72, 73, 78, 82, 84, 85, 86, 87, 89, 91, 93, 96, 99, 100, 111, 112, 113, 114, 116, 123, 125, 126, 128, 129, 130, 131, 133, 138, 139
white baneberry 91, 114, 120
white basswood 76
white blue-eyed grass 32
white butterfly 44
white chestnut 84
white clovers 63
white elm 38
white false indigo 121
white lady slipper orchid 12
white oak 20, 24, 27, 30, 35, 36, 40, 42, 52, 54, 55, 56, 64, 66, 68, 70, 72, 73, 74, 75, 76, 79, 80, 81, 82, 85, 86, 87, 88, 89, 90, 91, 92, 96, 97, 99, 100, 101, 102, 104, 105, 108, 110, 114, 116, 119, 121, 123, 128, 129, 131, 133, 134, 137, 138, 139
white pine 91, 96, 120
white poplar 131
white prairie lady slipper orchid 16
white rattlesnake 47
White's Branch Arch 96
white snakeroot 38, 52, 63, 111, 116
white sweet clover 9, 30, 102
white-tailed deer 11, 43
white trillium 40, 52, 91, 131
white trout lily 104, 113
white turtlehead 96
white walnut 24, 39, 52, 75, 82, 89
white warblers 83
Whitley Branch Wetland 134
Whitley County, Kentucky 21
whorled loosestrife 65
whorled milkweed 128
whorled rosinweed 128, 133
widow's cross 25, 54
wild bean 63
wild bergamot 32, 73
wild blue phlox 79, 89, 91
wild cherry 118
wild comfrey 52, 116, 139
Wilder, John T. 115
wildflower 20, 25, 27, 42, 79
wild geranium 27, 40, 69, 73, 84, 91, 123
wild ginger 22, 39, 52, 61, 63, 70, 72, 73, 84, 104, 126, 130
wild hyacinth 60, 113
wild hydrangea 39, 52, 66, 73, 104, 120, 128, 133
wild oats 77
wild petunia 132
wild quinine 121
wild rye grasses 60, 63, 68, 133
wild sweet william 120
wild turkeys 77
wild yam 87
Wilkins, Charles 29
William H. Martin Watershed and Wildlife Conservation Area 135
William Whitley House 136
willow oak 97, 134
winged elm 20, 49, 79, 86, 97, 128
winged sumac 99
wingstem 63
winterberry 27
winter creeper 9, 112
wintergreen 27, 120
witch hazel 37, 38, 81, 89, 92, 120, 126, 128
Wolfe County, Kentucky 120
wolves 16
wood anemone 27
wood ducks 23, 81
wood fern 119, 120
wood frogs 122
woodland phlox 52, 89
woodlands 29
woodland sunflower 87, 128
woodland wildflower 14
wood mint 74
wood nettle 38, 102, 116
wood poppy 39, 44, 84, 113, 116, 117, 126, 130, 139
wood rat 40
wood thrushes 83
woolly mammoths 29
Wooly Hemlock Adelgid 24
worm-eating warblers 83
worms 12
Wyatt Jefferies Woods 137

X

xeric calcareous woodland/forest 37
xeric oaks 21
xeric pine 21
xeric Virginia pine woodlands 37
xerohyridic flatwoods 26

Y

Yellowbank Wildlife Management Area 139
yellow birch 24, 69
yellow buckeye 24, 27, 38, 61, 69, 76, 82, 96, 123
Yellow Creek 138
Yellow Creek Park 138
Yellow fringed orchids 64
yellow gentian 30
yellow lady slipper orchids 40
yellow mandarin 27, 69, 92
yellow oak 77
yellow pine 65
Yellow-poplar 91
yellowroot 120
yellow screwstem 65
yellow star grass 79
yellow sweet clover 9
yellow trillium 36
yellow trout lily 34, 42, 44, 52, 60, 113
yellow wild indigo 65, 75
yellow wingstem 111
yellowwood 37, 85
young hemlocks 119
young sycamore 93

Z

zigzag goldenrod 27